Diving Into Parallel Universes

Diving Into Parallel Universes

Reality Reimagined

Ehsan Sheroy

UNIEK ENTERPRISES

CONTENTS

INDEX 1

Chapter 1 3

Chapter 2 17

Chapter 3 31

Chapter 4 43

Chapter 5 57

Chapter 6 73

Chapter 7 90

Chapter 8 104

Chapter 9 117

Chapter 1: Introduction to Parallel Universes
1.1 Defining parallel universes
1.2 Historical and philosophical background
1.3 The relevance of the multiverse concept

Chapter 2: The Many-Worlds Interpretation
2.1 Exploring Hugh Everett's Many-Worlds Interpretation
2.2 Quantum mechanics and branching realities
2.3 Implications for the nature of reality

Chapter 3: Quantum Entanglement and Parallel Realities
3.1 Understanding quantum entanglement
3.2 Theories of entanglement connecting parallel worlds
3.3 Experimental evidence and ongoing research

Chapter 4: Cosmic Microwave Background Radiation
4.1 The significance of CMB in cosmology
4.2 Hypotheses linking CMB to parallel universes
4.3 Ongoing efforts to detect evidence

Chapter 5: The Inflationary Multiverse
5.1 Cosmic inflation theory and the multiverse
5.2 Bubble universes and varying physical laws
5.3 Theoretical support and challenges

Chapter 6: Quantum Computing and Parallel Processing
6.1 Introduction to quantum computing
6.2 The potential impact on computational capabilities
6.3 Security challenges in a world of quantum computing

Chapter 7: Altered States of Consciousness
7.1 Meditation, psychedelics, and shamanic practices
7.2 Encounters with parallel dimensions
7.3 Expanding the boundaries of human awareness

Chapter 8: The Multiverse in Literature and Art
8.1 Science fiction narratives and the multiverse
8.2 The concept of the "mirror universe"
8.3 Parallel worlds in artistic expressions

Chapter 9: Contemplating the Boundless Possibilities
8.1 Reflection on the journey of exploration
8.2 The interconnectedness of events and choices
8.3 The enduring quest for understanding the mysteries of the cosmos

Chapter 1

Introduction to Parallel Universes

The idea of equal universes, otherwise called multiverse hypothesis, has spellbound the human creative mind for quite a long time. This fascinating thought recommends that there might be different universes, comparative or tremendously not quite the same as our own, existing together close by our existence. While the thought might appear to be implausible or the stuff of sci-fi, it has gotten some decent momentum in both hypothetical physical science and mainstream society. In this article, we will investigate the beginnings of the idea of equal universes, the different speculations that help their reality, and the ramifications these thoughts have on how we might interpret the universe.

One of the earliest recorded notices of equal universes can be followed back to antiquated Indian and Greek way of thinking. The Hindu idea of "Lila," meaning the heavenly play, places that our existence is only one of numerous indications of an enormous show. Essentially, the antiquated Greek thinker Anaximander suggested that there exist endless different universes in the universe. These early philosophical insights set up for future masterminds to dive into the possibility of different universes.

It was only after the twentieth century that the idea of equal universes acquired logical believability. Albert Einstein's hypothesis of general relativity, distributed in 1915, altered how we might interpret existence. It portrayed gravity as the shape of spacetime, taking into account the chance of twisted aspects and substitute real factors. While Einstein's hypothesis was historic, it didn't straightforwardly propose the presence of equal universes. All things considered, it established the groundwork for future work around here.

The main huge jump toward the idea of equal universes came from the field of quantum mechanics. In the mid twentieth 100 years, quantum physical science arose as a strong structure for grasping the way of behaving of subatomic particles.

This field presented the possibility that particles exist in various states until noticed, prompting the popular Schrödinger's feline psychological test, in which a feline could be both alive and dead at the same time. These quantum peculiarities provoked a few physicists to examine the presence of numerous real factors.

The "many-universes translation" of quantum mechanics, proposed by Hugh Everett III in 1957, is a fundamental hypothesis in the investigation of equal universes. As per this understanding, each quantum occasion with numerous potential results brings about the formation of equal universes, each expanding to oblige each conceivable result. Generally, it proposes that our universe is only one part of a boundlessly stretching tree of real factors. While the many-universes translation stays questionable, it offers a numerical system for figuring out the idea of equal universes.

Another unmistakable hypothesis supporting the presence of equal universes is the idea of grandiose expansion. Proposed by physicist Alan Guth in the mid 1980s, vast expansion recommends that the universe went through a quick extension in its initial minutes, during which various districts of room could form into particular universes. This hypothesis gives a component to producing countless equal universes, each with its special properties and actual regulations.

The presence of equal universes brings up significant issues about the idea of the real world and our place inside it. If the multiverse hypothesis is right, it intends that there are endless different renditions of us, carrying on with substitute lives in substitute real factors. This thought difficulties our traditional comprehension of uniqueness and selfhood, as it suggests that each conceivable decision and result is worked out in an equal universe.

Also, equal universes have critical ramifications for how we might interpret the universe. They might actually make sense of a portion of the secrets of the universe, for example, the tweaking of actual constants, which appear to be impeccably appropriate for the presence of life. In a multiverse, the thought is that we wind up in a universe with the right circumstances for life since it is just in such a universe that we could exist in any case. This idea has been known as the human-centered guideline.

Furthermore, the idea of equal universes has been investigated in mainstream society, particularly in sci-fi. Essayists and producers have utilized substitute real factors to recount convincing stories and investigate the human condition. Works like H.G. Wells' "The Time Machine" and Philip K. Dick's "The Man in the High Palace" have spellbound perusers and watchers with their portrayals of equal universes.

The topic of how one could demonstrate or negate the presence of equal universes stays a complicated and continuous test in the field of physical science. Since equal universes, by definition, exist past our noticeable universe, they are challenging to straightforwardly distinguish. In any case, physicists have proposed a few examinations and perceptions that could give roundabout proof to their reality.

One such road of investigation includes looking for peculiarities in the vast microwave foundation radiation (CMB), the luminosity of the Enormous detonation. Varieties in the CMB could be characteristic of different universes catching our own or having left engraves on our universe during their arrangement. Researchers are likewise concentrating on the circulation of cosmic systems and huge scope structures in the universe, looking for designs that could allude to the presence of different universes.

Another methodology includes concentrating on the way of behaving of particles at the quantum level. Assuming the many-universes understanding is exact, it very well might be feasible to notice quantum impedance designs that would be predictable with the presence of equal universes. Tests toward this path are testing and require very delicate gear, however they offer a possible road for exact proof.

Besides, continuous exploration in hypothetical physical science is investigating the chance of "brane universes." These are multi-faceted designs in which our universe is only one of many "branes" drifting in a higher-layered space. Impacts or collaborations between these branes could lead to resemble universes or leave recognizable follows in our universe.

The thought of equal universes likewise has suggestions for probably the most significant inquiries in cosmology and reasoning. For instance, whether or not our universe is interesting or only one of many has significant ramifications for the quest for extraterrestrial life. Assuming our universe is one of endless others, it improves the probability that life has arisen somewhere else, possibly in structures that we couldn't envision.

The presence of equal universes likewise brings up issues about the idea of awareness and oneself. On the off chance that each conceivable result of each and every quantum occasion happens in an equal universe, it recommends that each decision we make prompts a spreading of real factors. This prompts the topic of what "you" signifies in a multiverse. Is it safe to say that you are the amount of every one of your decisions across this multitude of universes, or would you say you are only one rendition of yourself among endless others?

Equal universes can likewise reveal insight into the idea of time and causality. Assuming each conceivable result is acknowledged in an equal universe, does this imply that the idea of circumstances and logical results becomes old? What's the significance here with the expectation of complimentary will in the event that each conceivable decision is worked out in various universes? These inquiries challenge how we might interpret central parts of presence.

Notwithstanding the philosophical and logical ramifications, equal universes have enamored the human creative mind through different types of workmanship and narrating. Sci-fi has been especially prolific ground for investigating the idea of substitute real factors. Creators and producers have utilized equal universes to make complex and provocative stories that dig into the human condition and the outcomes of our decisions.

The idea of equal universes has additionally impacted the field of speculative fiction, prompting the production of subgenres like substitute history and equal world fiction. Works like Philip K. Dick's "The Man in the High Palace" investigate equal universes where authentic situation developed in an unexpected way, bringing up issues about the idea of the real world and the effect of decisions on the course of history.

In writing and film, equal universes have given a rich scenery to investigating subjects of personality and self-revelation. Stories frequently include characters who experience substitute renditions of themselves, inciting reflections on their decisions and the ways not taken. These stories challenge how we might interpret uniqueness and the idea that there is a solitary "valid" self.

Besides, equal universes have been utilized to analyze the results of human activities and moral problems. By introducing substitute real factors where various decisions were made, creators and producers can investigate the likely results of choices and the ethical ramifications of those decisions.

All in all, the idea of equal universes, however once restricted to the domains of reasoning and sci-fi, has gotten some decent forward momentum in the field of hypothetical physical science and mainstream society. From its initial roots in antiquated way of thinking to present day translations in quantum mechanics and astronomical expansion, the possibility of different universes existing close by our own has fascinated humankind for quite a long time.

The investigation of equal universes can possibly rethink how we might interpret reality, uniqueness, and the actual universe. While the proof for their reality stays tricky and speculative, progressing research and hypothetical improvements keep on pushing the limits of our insight and challenge our most crucial suspicions about the universe.

The idea of equal universes brings up significant issues about the idea of the real world and our place inside it. If the multiverse hypothesis is right, it intends that there are endless different adaptations of us, carrying on with substitute lives in substitute real factors. This thought difficulties our regular comprehension of uniqueness and selfhood, as it suggests that each conceivable decision and result is worked out in an equal universe.

Also, equal universes have huge ramifications for how we might interpret the universe. They might actually make sense of a portion of the secrets of the universe, for example, the tweaking of actual constants, which appear to be impeccably appropriate for the presence of life. In a multiverse, the thought is that we end up in a universe with the right circumstances for life since it is just in such a universe that we could exist in any case. This thought has been known as the human-centered rule.

Furthermore, the idea of equal universes has been investigated in mainstream society, particularly in sci-fi. Journalists and movie producers have utilized substitute real factors to recount convincing stories and investigate the human condition. Works like H.G. Wells' "The Time Machine" and Philip K. Dick's "The Man in the High Palace" have spellbound perusers and watchers with their portrayals of equal universes.

The topic of how one could demonstrate or negate the presence of equal universes stays a complicated and continuous test in the field of material science. Since equal universes, by definition, exist past our recognizable universe, they are challenging to straightforwardly distinguish. Nonetheless, physicists have proposed a few trials and perceptions that could give circuitous proof to their reality.

One such road of investigation includes looking for peculiarities in the enormous microwave foundation radiation (CMB), the phosphorescence of the Huge explosion. Varieties in the CMB could be characteristic of different universes finding our own or having left engraves on our universe during their development. Researchers are additionally concentrating on the appropriation of cosmic systems and huge scope structures in the universe, looking for designs that could allude to the presence of different universes.

Another methodology includes concentrating on the way of behaving of particles at the quantum level. Assuming the many-universes understanding is exact, it very well might be feasible to notice quantum impedance designs that would be reliable with the presence of equal universes. Tests toward this path are testing and require incredibly touchy gear, however they offer an expected road for observational proof.

Moreover, continuous exploration in hypothetical material science is investigating the chance of "brane universes." These are multi-layered structures in which our universe is only one of many "branes" drifting in a higher-layered space. Crashes or cooperations between these branes could lead to resemble universes or leave perceptible follows in our universe.

The thought of equal universes additionally has suggestions for the absolute most significant inquiries in cosmology and reasoning. For instance, whether or not our universe is interesting or only one of many has significant ramifications for the quest for extraterrestrial life. Assuming our universe is one of endless others, it improves the probability that life has arisen somewhere else, possibly in structures that we couldn't actually envision.

The presence of equal universes likewise brings up issues about the idea of awareness and oneself. On the off chance that each conceivable result of each and every quantum occasion happens in an equal universe, it recommends that each decision we make prompts a fanning of real factors. This prompts the subject of what "you" signifies in a multiverse. Could it be said that you are the amount of every one of your decisions across this multitude of universes, or would you say you are only one form of yourself among endless others?

Equal universes can likewise reveal insight into the idea of time and causality. Assuming that each conceivable result is acknowledged in an equal universe, does this imply that the idea of circumstances and logical results becomes old? What's the significance here with the expectation of complimentary will assuming each conceivable decision is worked out in various universes? These inquiries challenge how we might interpret essential parts of presence.

Notwithstanding the philosophical and logical ramifications, equal universes have enamored the human creative mind through different types of workmanship and narrating. Sci-fi has been especially ripe ground for investigating the idea of substitute real factors. Creators and movie producers have utilized equal universes to make complex and interesting accounts that dig into the human condition and the outcomes of our decisions.

The idea of equal universes has additionally affected the field of speculative fiction, prompting the making of subgenres like substitute history and equal world fiction. Works like Philip K. Dick's "The Man in the High Palace" investigate equal universes where authentic situation transpired in an unexpected way, bringing up issues about the idea of the real world and the effect of decisions on the course of history.

In writing and film, equal universes have given a rich setting to investigating subjects of character and self-revelation. Stories frequently include characters who experience substitute variants of themselves, inciting reflections on their decisions and the ways not taken. These stories challenge how we might interpret independence and the idea that there is a solitary "valid" self.

Besides, equal universes have been utilized to inspect the outcomes of human activities and moral predicaments. By introducing substitute real factors where various decisions were made, creators and producers can investigate the likely results of choices and the ethical ramifications of those decisions.

1.1 Defining parallel universes

The idea of equal universes, otherwise called the multiverse, is an interesting and complex thought that has caught the creative mind of researchers, savants, and journalists for quite a long time. It proposes the presence of different universes, particular from our own, that might have different actual regulations, chronicles, and even varieties in the major constants of nature. The thought of equal universes challenges our regular comprehension of the real world and brings up significant issues about the idea of the universe, our place inside it, and the major rules that oversee the universe.

One of the essential thoughts behind the idea of equal universes is that the universe we possess is only one of numerous potential universes. These different universes can change in endless ways, offering a tremendous scene of expected real factors.

To dive further into the idea of equal universes, it is fundamental to analyze its beginnings, various hypotheses and models, the proof, or scarcity in that department, for their reality, and the philosophical ramifications these thoughts involve.

The Starting points of the Idea

Equal universes has its underlying foundations in different philosophical and strict practices. Old Hindu way of thinking, for example, presented the idea of "Lila," the heavenly play, which recommends that the universe is a great show with numerous signs and real factors. Along these lines, antiquated Greek rationalists pondered the presence of various universes or universes, accepting that there may be different Earths in the tremendous universe.

These early philosophical insights set up for later masterminds and researchers to investigate the idea of equal universes. While these early thoughts were many times speculative and established in mystical or profound convictions, they established the groundwork for a more thorough and logical assessment of the thought in the cutting edge period.

Logical Turn of events

The twentieth century saw critical advancements in material science that laid the foundation for the idea of equal universes to acquire logical believability. Albert Einstein's hypothesis of general relativity, distributed in 1915, upset how we might interpret gravity and space-time. It presented distorted space-time, which considered the chance of substitute real factors and different aspects.

While Einstein's hypothesis of general relativity didn't straightforwardly propose the presence of equal universes, it prepared for later advancements in hypothetical material science and cosmology that would investigate these conceivable outcomes all the more completely.

Quite possibly of the most persuasive field in the investigation of equal universes is quantum mechanics. Quantum physical science, which arose in the mid twentieth hundred years, gave another structure to figuring out the way of behaving of particles at the subatomic level. Fundamental to this field is the idea of superposition, which recommends that particles can exist in numerous states all the while until they are noticed. This thought was broadly epitomized in Schrödinger's feline psychological test, in which a feline could be both alive and dead until noticed.

These quantum peculiarities, which tested traditional ideas of determinism and causality, drove a few physicists to examine the presence of different real factors. Whether or not particles can exist in that frame of mind without a moment's delay normally raised the chance of various universes or real factors coinciding.

Many-Universes Understanding

The "many-universes understanding" of quantum mechanics, proposed by physicist Hugh Everett III in 1957, is a basic hypothesis in the investigation of equal universes. As per this translation, each quantum occasion with numerous potential results brings about the making of equal universes. Fundamentally, every conceivable result of a quantum occasion is acknowledged in a different universe.

For instance, in the event that you were confronted with a decision between following some way, in a many-universes situation, the two decisions would prompt the making of discrete universes. One universe would go on with the outcomes of your best option, and one more universe would investigate the consequences of your subsequent option. This translation recommends that our universe is only one part of a boundlessly stretching tree of real factors.

The many-universes translation offers a numerical structure for figuring out the idea of equal universes inside the setting of quantum mechanics. It attests that all potential results happen, and each is similarly truly in its particular universe. While the many-universes translation stays dubious and includes elective understandings inside the field of quantum mechanics, it plays had a huge impact in molding how we might interpret equal universes.

Grandiose Expansion

Another noticeable hypothesis supporting the presence of equal universes is the idea of infinite expansion. Proposed by physicist Alan Guth in the mid 1980s, enormous expansion recommends that the universe went through a fast and dramatic extension in its initial minutes. This extension might have made various locales of room with particular properties, prompting the development of independent universes.

With regards to astronomical expansion, locales of room with various energy levels can bring about universes with varieties in their actual regulations and constants. This hypothesis gives a component to producing countless equal universes, each with its novel arrangement of properties. Enormous expansion has acquired help from galactic perceptions and has turned into a fundamental part of the Theory of the universe's origin.

The Ramifications of Equal Universes

The idea of equal universes conveys significant ramifications for how we might interpret the universe, the idea of the real world, and our place inside it. One of the most captivating parts of the multiverse speculation is the possibility that there are endless different forms of us, carrying on with substitute lives in equal real factors.

This idea challenges our ordinary thoughts of uniqueness and selfhood. In the event that each conceivable decision and result is worked out in an equal universe, it brings up the issue of being an individual and whether there is a solitary "valid" self. It prompts philosophical investigations into the idea of character, individual decisions, and the idea of self with regards to a multiverse.

In addition, equal universes might possibly reveal insight into a portion of the secrets of the universe. The calibrating of actual constants and the clear appropriateness of the universe for the development of life have for quite some time been subjects of logical request. In a multiverse, the human-centered standard proposes that we end up in a universe with the right circumstances for life since it is just in such a universe that we could exist in any case.

The human-centered guideline places that the circumstances in our universe are a consequence of choice predisposition. Life, and likewise, smart onlookers such as ourselves, can exist in universes where the actual constants and conditions are appropriate for life to arise. This brings up the issue of whether the universe is calibrated for our reality or on the other hand on the off chance that our reality is a result of the universe's boundaries.

The presence of equal universes additionally has suggestions for the quest for extraterrestrial life. Assuming our universe is only one of endless others, it improves the probability that life might have arisen somewhere else, possibly in structures and conditions that are unfathomably not the same as our own. The possibility that we could one day find other clever developments inside the multiverse challenges our viewpoint on the uniqueness of humankind and our position in the universe.

Proof and Difficulties

While the idea of equal universes is a charming and mentally invigorating thought, whether or not they exist stays a subject of continuous discussion and examination. Demonstrating or invalidating the presence of equal universes is a perplexing and testing try.

One of the essential hardships in concentrating on equal universes is that they, by definition, exist past our detectable universe. This implies that any immediate proof of their reality is slippery and may remain perpetually past our span. In any case, physicists and cosmologists have proposed a few roundabout strategies and tests that could give proof or backing to the multiverse speculation.

Irregularities in the Vast Microwave Foundation (CMB): The grandiose microwave foundation radiation is the luminosity of the Huge explosion, and it gives significant experiences into the early universe. Varieties in the CMB could be demonstrative of different universes brushing against our own or leaving engraves on our universe during their development. Researchers are effectively looking for abnormalities in the CMB that could allude to the presence of different universes.

Dispersion of Systems and Huge Scope Designs: The conveyance of worlds and enormous scope structures in the universe can likewise offer hints about the presence of equal universes.

A few speculations recommend that the gravitational impact of adjoining universes might leave discernible examples in the conveyance of systems. By breaking down the enormous scope construction of the universe, analysts plan to recognize any uncommon examples or irregularities that could be connected to different universes.

Quantum Mechanics and the Many-Universes Understanding: Assuming the many-universes translation of quantum mechanics is right, it very well might be feasible to notice quantum impedance designs that line up with the presence of equal universes. Tests toward this path are testing and require incredibly touchy gear, yet they offer a likely road for exact proof.

1.2 Historical and philosophical background

The idea of equal universes, or the multiverse, is well established in mankind's set of experiences and reasoning, crossing many social and scholarly practices. To comprehend the contemporary conversations and hypotheses encompassing equal universes, it is fundamental to investigate their verifiable and philosophical forerunners, which have added to molding the manner in which we ponder substitute real factors and the universe.

Antiquated Philosophical and Strict Customs

Equal universes has its starting points in the philosophical and strict customs of different old societies. These early thoughts established the groundwork for later masterminds to investigate the idea in more profundity.

In Hindu way of thinking, the idea of "Lila" or the heavenly play proposes that the universe is a fantastic show with numerous signs and real factors. Inside this perspective, the truth is viewed as a perplexing transaction of heavenly powers, with every reality or sign addressing a novel feature of presence. The possibility of Lila presents a variety of universes and aspects, indicating the chance of equal universes.

Also, old Greek thinkers mulled over the presence of various universes or universes. The thinker Anaximander, for instance, guessed that different universes could exist in the limitlessness of the universe. These early philosophical requests were many times speculative and needed exact help, yet they set up for later improvements in the idea of equal universes.

In these early customs, equal universes was frequently entwined with supernatural or strict convictions, mirroring mankind's significant interest in the idea of presence and the universe.

The Edification and the Introduction of Present day Science

The Logical Transformation of the sixteenth and seventeenth hundreds of years, which denoted a takeoff from customary strict and philosophical perspectives, laid the basis for additional efficient and exact investigations of the universe.

Rationalists and researchers started to move their concentration from magical and philosophical inquiries to the investigation of the regular world.

During this period, historic figures like Galileo Galilei and Johannes Kepler mentioned basic observable facts and planned regulations that upset comprehension we might interpret the universe. The heliocentric model of the planetary group, created by Copernicus and refined by Kepler and Galileo, dislodged the Earth from its focal position, uncovering an immense universe with heavenly bodies that were once remembered to be heavenly or outside human ability to grasp.

Isaac Newton's laws of movement and widespread attractive energy gave a rational structure to grasping the way of behaving of items in the universe. These logical advances denoted the change from a geocentric and human-centric perspective to a more extensive, robotic, and naturalistic viewpoint on the universe.

While these improvements were crucial in propelling comprehension we might interpret the universe, they didn't straightforwardly address the idea of equal universes. Nonetheless, they established the groundwork for a more experimental and proof based way to deal with investigating the universe, which would become essential in later conversations of equal universes.

The Ascent of Present day Way of thinking and Power

As logical information extended, savants in the seventeenth and eighteenth hundreds of years wrestled with the ramifications of these revelations for how we might interpret reality and the idea of presence. René Descartes, for example, underscored the dualism of brain and body, bringing up issues about the connection between the physical and non-actual parts of the real world.

Immanuel Kant's philosophical works, especially his "Scrutinize of Unadulterated Explanation," investigated the limits of human information and the restrictions of our comprehension. Kant's thoughts significantly affected power, epistemology, and the way of thinking of science, as he contended that specific parts of reality may be past human discernment and appreciation.

It was during this time that the idea of equal universes started to reappear in philosophical conversations. The logician Gottfried Wilhelm Leibniz, known for his work on math and his powerful requests, presented the idea of the "monad." Monads were indissoluble, non-material substances that make up the texture of the real world. Leibniz's supernatural system proposed that each monad addressed an extraordinary viewpoint on the universe, and that there may be a boundless number of monads, each comparing to an alternate conceivable world.

Leibniz's thoughts, however profoundly unique and powerful, set up for later philosophical investigations of equal universes. The idea that there may be various potential universes, each with its unmistakable situation, would turn into a vital component in the improvement of the idea of equal universes.

1.3 The relevance of the multiverse concept

The idea of equal universes, otherwise called the multiverse, has acquired expanding noticeable quality in contemporary logical and philosophical talk. This idea has produced huge interest and discussion, fundamentally because of its capability to address the absolute most significant inquiries in cosmology, physical science, and reasoning. As how we might interpret the universe and its major standards develops, the multiverse idea offers a system for investigating complex issues and gives new points of view on the idea of the real world and our place inside it.

The importance of the multiverse idea can be grasped through its effect on different parts of science, reasoning, and, surprisingly, the more extensive social and scholarly scene. In this conversation, we will investigate the critical spaces where the multiverse idea assumes a huge part and the ramifications it has for how we might interpret the universe.

Cosmology and the Idea of the Universe:

The multiverse idea has huge ramifications for how we might interpret the universe and the crucial idea of the universe. Quite possibly of the most significant inquiry in cosmology is the supposed "tweaking issue." It connects with the exceptional accuracy of the crucial actual constants and conditions in our universe, which have all the earmarks of being finely tuned to permit the development of life. The multiverse idea gives an expected answer for this issue.

As per the human-centered guideline, which is firmly connected with the multiverse idea, our universe's circumstances are a consequence of choice inclination. Life, and likewise, keen spectators such as ourselves, can exist in universes with actual constants and conditions reasonable forever. In a multiverse, the thought is that we end up in a universe with the right circumstances for life since it is just in such a universe that we could exist in any case. This thought brings up issues about whether our universe is tweaked for our reality or on the other hand on the off chance that our reality is a result of the universe's boundaries.

The multiverse idea offers another viewpoint on the calibrating issue by proposing that the obvious tweaking may not be so impossible assuming there are endless different universes with fluctuating actual regulations and constants. In this specific situation, our universe's exceptional circumstances should be visible as a result of the huge scene of conceivable outcomes inside the multiverse.

Astrobiology and the Quest for Extraterrestrial Life:

The presence of equal universes likewise has suggestions for the quest for extra-terrestrial life. Assuming our universe is only one of endless others, it improves the probability that life might have arisen somewhere else, possibly in structures and conditions that are immeasurably unique in relation to our own.

The possibility that we could one day find other savvy developments inside the multiverse challenges our viewpoint on the uniqueness of mankind and our spot in the universe.

With regards to astrobiology, the multiverse idea prompts scientists to consider the more extensive scope of conceivable living things and conditions that could exist in different universes. It empowers a more broad perspective on the circumstances that could uphold life and the structures that life could take. While this investigation stays speculative, it shows the multiverse's pertinence in extending our contemplating the possible variety of life past Earth.

Quantum Mechanics and the Many-Universes Translation:

Quantum mechanics, with its inborn probabilistic and indeterministic nature, has been a wellspring of interest and perplexity for physicists and scholars the same. The multiverse idea, explicitly the many-universes translation, offers an elective method for figuring out quantum peculiarities.

In the many-universes understanding, each quantum occasion with different potential results brings about the making of equal universes. This translation recommends that all potential results happen, and each is similarly truly in its separate universe. It challenges ordinary thoughts regarding the breakdown of the quantum wave capability and the idea that a solitary not entirely settled by perception.

The pertinence of the many-universes translation lies in its capability to give a more cognizant and extensive structure for understanding the way of behaving of particles at the quantum level. It offers a point of view where quantum superposition isn't simply a numerical deliberation yet mirrors the presence of numerous, fanning real factors. This translation keeps on molding conversations in quantum mechanics and the way of thinking of science.

Reasoning and the Idea of The real world:

The multiverse idea has significant ramifications for philosophical investigations into the idea of the real world, distinction, and oneself. Assuming each conceivable result of each and every quantum occasion happens in an equal universe, it suggests that each decision we make prompts a stretching of real factors. This brings up the issue of what "you" signifies in a multiverse. Is it true that you are the amount of every one of your decisions across this multitude of universes, or would you say you are only one form of yourself among incalculable others?

Savants have drawn in with these inquiries, investigating the idea of character and individual organization inside the multiverse structure. It challenges conventional thoughts of determinism and through and through freedom, as well as the idea of causality. In a multiverse, the idea of circumstances and logical results turns out to be more mind boggling, as each conceivable decision and result coincide in discrete real factors.

Moreover, the multiverse idea welcomes philosophical reflections on the idea of presence and the meaning of individual decisions. It prompts contemplations about the relativity of profound quality, morals, and the outcomes of choices. In this specific circumstance, the multiverse turns into a fruitful ground for investigating complex moral predicaments and the relativity of moral decisions.

Sci-fi and Mainstream society:

The idea of equal universes has pervaded mainstream society, particularly in the domain of sci-fi. Works of writing, film, and TV have utilized substitute real factors to make complex stories and investigate a great many subjects, from personality and self-revelation to moral and moral situations.

Sci-fi has been a strong vehicle for acquainting the multiverse idea with a more extensive crowd. Works like H.G. Wells' "The Time Machine" and Philip K. Dick's "The Man in the High Palace" have spellbound perusers and watchers with their portrayals of equal universes. These accounts engage as well as incite suspected on the ramifications of decisions and the relativity of the real world.

The impact of the multiverse in mainstream society reaches out to video games, where players frequently explore substitute real factors and go with decisions that influence the game's result. This intuitive type of narrating permits players to encounter the idea of equal universes firsthand and investigate the outcomes of their choices.

Taking everything into account, the importance of the multiverse idea traverses various spaces, from cosmology and reasoning to sci-fi and mainstream society. This idea offers new viewpoints on key inquiries concerning the idea of the universe, the tweaking of actual constants, the quest for extraterrestrial life, the way of behaving of particles at the quantum level, and the idea of the real world and uniqueness.

While the multiverse idea stays a subject of continuous examination and discussion, its effect on these different areas of human request is obvious. The multiverse challenges our customary comprehension of the real world and offers a system for investigating complex issues and philosophical inquiries that have charmed humankind for quite a long time. It keeps on moving inventive exploration and innovative narrating, extending our points of view and developing our enthusiasm for the secrets of the universe.

Chapter 2

The Many-Worlds Interpretation

The Many-Universes Translation (MWI) of quantum mechanics is an unmistakable and provocative hypothesis that has enamored the consideration of physicists, scholars, and science devotees for quite a long time. First proposed by Hugh Everett III in 1957, the MWI offers an extreme point of view on the idea of the real world and the way of behaving of particles at the quantum level. This understanding recommends that each quantum occasion with different potential results brings about the production of equal universes, each fanning out to oblige each likely result. In this conversation, we will investigate the critical standards and ramifications of the Many-Universes Translation, as well as the continuous discussions and difficulties it postures to how we might interpret the quantum domain and the universe.

Standards of the Many-Universes Translation:

Quantum Superposition: Vital to the Many-Universes Translation is the idea of quantum superposition. In quantum mechanics, particles, for example, electrons and photons are portrayed as existing in a mix of different states or positions all the while until they are noticed or estimated. This superposition of states is a major part of quantum physical science and difficulties traditional thoughts of determinism.

Expanding Universes: As per the Many-Universes Translation, when a quantum occasion has numerous potential results, every one of these results prompts the formation of a different part of the real world. These branches are frequently alluded to as "universes" or "universes." at the end of the day, each conceivable consequence of a quantum occasion is acknowledged in an alternate universe.

Wave Capability: The wave capability in quantum mechanics addresses the likelihood dissemination of a molecule's states. In the Many-Universes Understanding, the wave capability doesn't implode as it does in that frame of mind of quantum mechanics.

All things being equal, it keeps on developing, leading to numerous parts of the real world, each comparing to an alternate result.

Concurrence of Real factors: Significantly, the Many-Universes Translation affirms that these equal universes are similarly genuine. In every universe, the result of the quantum occasion is clear, and the related the truth is as "genuine" as our own. This translation challenges the idea of a solitary, objective reality and proposes that various real factors exist together.

Ramifications of the Many-Universes Understanding:

The Many-Universes Translation has sweeping ramifications for how we might interpret quantum mechanics, the idea of the real world, and our place inside the universe. Here are a portion of the vital ramifications and areas of significance:

Goal of the Estimation Issue: One of the focal issues in quantum mechanics is the estimation issue, which relates to the puzzling breakdown of the wave capability upon estimation. The Many-Universes Translation gives a rich answer for this issue. Rather than a breakdown, the wave capability keeps on developing, with every conceivable result prompting the formation of another universe. This translation wipes out the requirement for hypothesizing a different cycle for wave capability breakdown.

Determinism versus Indeterminism: The Many-Universes Translation challenges the customary division among determinism and indeterminism. While it recognizes that quantum occasions are probabilistic and uncertain at the quantum level, it states that the advancement of the wave capability is deterministic. In this structure, each conceivable result is understood, and the development of the wave capability is administered by deterministic conditions.

Understanding of Quantum Examinations: The Many-Universes Translation gives an alternate point of view on the results of quantum tests. It proposes that when an estimation is made, it isn't simply uncovering a previous reality yet deciding the result in the eyewitness' part of the universe. This has significant ramifications for the job of spectators in quantum tests and the idea of quantum reality.

Quantum Trap: Quantum snare, a peculiarity where particles become related so that the condition of one molecule is reliant upon the condition of another, is a basic part of quantum mechanics. The Many-Universes Translation offers a special point of view on ensnarement. In this structure, trapped particles are not conveying across space promptly, as recommended by different translations, yet rather their states become related because of their common history in a similar part of the universe prior to stretching happens.

Quantum Figuring: The Many-Universes Translation has suggestions for quantum registering, a field that takes advantage of the standards of quantum mechanics to perform calculations at speeds unthinkable for old style PCs.

Quantum PCs depend on the possibility of superposition, and the MWI gives an original point of view on how quantum calculations work. The idea of equal universes coinciding permits quantum PCs to investigate different arrangements at the same time, possibly upsetting the field of calculation.

Philosophical Ramifications: The Many-Universes Understanding has significant philosophical ramifications. It challenges our customary ideas of the real world, personality, and singularity. In a multiverse with stretching universes, the idea of "self" turns out to be more mind boggling, as each decision and result lead to the formation of various variants of oneself. It prompts philosophical investigations into the idea of character, individual decisions, and the idea of self with regards to a multiverse.

Moral and Moral Contemplations: equal universes brings up moral and moral issues connected with the outcomes of activities. In a multiverse, the results of decisions and activities are worked out in various real factors. This has suggestions for the relativity of profound quality and the meaning of individual decisions. It prompts contemplations about the relativity of morals and the outcomes of choices.

Discussions and Difficulties:

The Many-Universes Translation, in spite of its reasonable style and illustrative power, stays a subject of discussion and countenances a few difficulties:

The Issue of Likelihood: Pundits contend that the Many-Universes Understanding brings up issues about the translation of probabilities in quantum mechanics. In a multiverse, the possibility of likelihood turns out to be more complicated, as all potential results are understood. Some battle that this difficulties the traditional comprehension of likelihood and its association with the recurrence of occasions.

Testability and Exact Proof: The Many-Universes Translation is frequently reprimanded for its clear absence of experimental testability. As equal universes are, by definition, distant to coordinate perception, some contend that the MWI misses the mark regarding the logical rule of observational confirmation. Notwithstanding, advocates of the MWI highlight roundabout tests, like those connected with quantum snare and the way of behaving of particles, as possible proof.

Ontological Responsibility: Pundits likewise bring up issues about the ontological responsibility of the Many-Universes Understanding. They contend that the proposition of a boundless number of equal universes may be viewed as luxurious or superfluous, as different understandings of quantum mechanics give similarly legitimate portrayals of quantum peculiarities without summoning a multiverse.

Soundness of Spreading: A few studies question the lucidness of the idea of expanding universes. They contend that it is indistinct how the parting of reality happens, what decides while stretching occurs, and whether there is an ordered progression of fanning. These inquiries challenge the applied clearness of the MWI.

Elective Understandings: Quantum mechanics offers numerous translations, each with its own benefits and difficulties. While the Many-Universes Understanding is quite possibly of the most examined, other translation, for example, the Copenhagen understanding and the pilot-wave hypothesis, give alternate points of view on quantum peculiarities. The decision of understanding remaining parts a question of progressing discussion and individual inclination among physicists and rationalists.

2.1 Exploring Hugh Everett's Many-Worlds Interpretation

Hugh Everett III's Many-Universes Understanding (MWI) of quantum mechanics is quite possibly of the most captivating and dubious hypothesis in the field of material science and reasoning. First proposed in 1957, the MWI challenges how we might interpret the quantum world and the idea of reality itself. This translation sets that each quantum occasion with different potential results brings about the formation of equal universes, each expanding to oblige each expected result. In this conversation, we will dive into the key standards, authentic setting, suggestions, and reactions of the Many-Universes Understanding.

Authentic Setting and Advancement:

To see the value in the meaning of the Many-Universes Translation, it is fundamental to comprehend the authentic setting wherein it arose. During the twentieth 100 years, quantum mechanics had previously secured itself as a strong and effective structure for grasping the way of behaving of particles at the nuclear and subatomic levels. In any case, there were waiting inquiries and difficulties inside the hypothesis, especially in regards to the estimation issue and the idea of wave capability breakdown.

The estimation issue rotated around the strange and apparently inconsistent breakdown of the quantum wave capability upon estimation. This cycle, as portrayed in different understandings of quantum mechanics, brought about a solitary result, leaving unanswered inquiries regarding the reason why and how this breakdown happened.

In this unique circumstance, Hugh Everett III, a youthful physicist seeking after his doctoral examinations at Princeton College, tried to resolve these issues. Everett's doctoral exposition, named "Relative State Definition of Quantum Mechanics," introduced a novel and revolutionary translation of quantum mechanics. In this translation, he suggested that as opposed to the wave capability imploding to a solitary result, it kept on developing, leading to different parts of the real world.

The MWI was met with blended responses inside the material science local area at that point. While a perceived its calculated tastefulness and capacity to determine the estimation issue, others were incredulous and found it trying to acknowledge the possibility of a multiverse. In any case, the MWI endured and has turned into a huge subject of conversation and discussion in the domains of quantum mechanics and the way of thinking of science.

Key Standards of the Many-Universes Understanding:

Quantum Superposition: Integral to the Many-Universes Understanding is the idea of quantum superposition. In quantum mechanics, particles, for example, electrons and photons are depicted as existing in a blend of various states or positions at the same time until they are noticed or estimated. This superposition of states is a major part of quantum physical science.

Expanding Universes: As per the Many-Universes Translation, when a quantum occasion has different potential results, every one of these results prompts the formation of a different part of the real world. These branches are frequently alluded to as "universes" or "universes." as such, every conceivable consequence of a quantum occasion is acknowledged in an alternate universe.

Wave Capability: The wave capability in quantum mechanics addresses the likelihood conveyance of a molecule's states. In the Many-Universes Translation, the wave capability doesn't fall as it does in that frame of mind of quantum mechanics. All things being equal, it keeps on developing, leading to various parts of the real world, each comparing to an alternate result.

Conjunction of Real factors: Critically, the Many-Universes Understanding affirms that these equal universes are similarly genuine. In every universe, the result of the quantum occasion is unequivocal, and the related the truth is as "genuine" as our own. This understanding difficulties the idea of a solitary, objective reality and proposes that various real factors exist together.

Ramifications of the Many-Universes Understanding:

The Many-Universes Translation has significant ramifications for how we might interpret quantum mechanics, the idea of the real world, and our place inside the universe. Here are a portion of the critical ramifications and areas of significance:

Goal of the Estimation Issue: The Many-Universes Understanding gives an extraordinary and rich answer for the estimation issue in quantum mechanics. In the MWI, the wave capability doesn't implode upon estimation; all things considered, it keeps on developing, with every conceivable result prompting the making of another universe. This disposes of the requirement for hypothesizing a different cycle for wave capability breakdown.

Determinism versus Indeterminism: The Many-Universes Translation challenges the conventional division among determinism and indeterminism. While it recognizes that quantum occasions are probabilistic and vague at the quantum level, it states that the advancement of the wave capability is deterministic. In this structure, each conceivable result is understood, and the development of the wave capability is administered by deterministic conditions.

Translation of Quantum Examinations: The Many-Universes Understanding gives an alternate point of view on the results of quantum tests. It recommends that when an estimation is made, it isn't simply uncovering a prior the real world yet deciding the result in the eyewitness' part of the universe. This has significant ramifications for the job of onlookers in quantum tests and the idea of quantum reality.

Quantum Trap: Quantum entrapment, a peculiarity where particles become corresponded so that the condition of one molecule is subject to the condition of another, is a principal part of quantum mechanics. The Many-Universes Understanding offers a novel point of view on ensnarement. In this system, snared particles are not conveying across space promptly, as recommended by different understandings, yet rather their states become connected because of their common history in a similar part of the universe prior to spreading happens.

Quantum Figuring: The Many-Universes Understanding has suggestions for quantum registering, a field that takes advantage of the standards of quantum mechanics to perform calculations at speeds incomprehensible for old style PCs. Quantum PCs depend on the possibility of superposition, and the MWI gives an original point of view on how quantum calculations work. In the idea of equal universes existing together, quantum PCs can investigate different arrangements at the same time, possibly reforming the field of calculation.

Philosophical Ramifications: The Many-Universes Understanding has significant philosophical ramifications. It challenges our customary ideas of the real world, character, and singularity. In a multiverse with stretching universes, the idea of "self" turns out to be more complicated, as each decision and result lead to the formation of various variants of oneself. It prompts philosophical investigations into the idea of character, individual decisions, and the idea of self with regards to a multiverse.

Moral and Moral Contemplations: equal universes brings up moral and moral issues connected with the results of activities. In a multiverse, the results of decisions and activities are worked out in various real factors. This has suggestions for the relativity of profound quality and the meaning of individual decisions. It prompts contemplations about the relativity of morals and the outcomes of choices.

Reactions and Difficulties:

The Many-Universes Understanding, regardless of its calculated tastefulness and informative power, stays a subject of discussion and countenances a few reactions and difficulties:

The Issue of Likelihood: Pundits contend that the Many-Universes Understanding brings up issues about the translation of probabilities in quantum mechanics. In a multiverse, the possibility of likelihood turns out to be more complicated, as all potential results are understood. Some fight that this difficulties the customary comprehension of likelihood and its association with the recurrence of occasions.

Testability and Experimental Proof: The Many-Universes Understanding is frequently reprimanded for its evident absence of exact testability. As equal universes are, by definition, difficult to reach to coordinate perception, some contend that the MWI misses the mark concerning the logical basis of exact check. Notwithstanding, defenders of the MWI highlight roundabout tests, like those connected with quantum ensnarement and the way of behaving of particles, as possible proof.

Ontological Responsibility: Pundits likewise bring up issues about the ontological responsibility of the Many-Universes Translation. They contend that the proposition of a boundless number of equal universes may be viewed as lavish or pointless, as different understandings of quantum mechanics give similarly substantial portrayals of quantum peculiarities without summoning a multiverse.

Cognizance of Fanning: A few investigates question the intelligibility of the idea of stretching universes. It is indistinct how the parting of reality happens, what decides while fanning occurs, and whether there is an ordered progression of stretching. These inquiries challenge the reasonable clearness of the MWI.

Elective Translations: Quantum mechanics offers various understandings, each with its own benefits and difficulties. While the Many-Universes Understanding is quite possibly of the most examined, other translation, for example, the Copenhagen translation and the pilot-wave hypothesis, give alternate points of view on quantum peculiarities. The decision of translation stays an issue of continuous discussion and individual inclination among physicists and thinkers.

2.2 Quantum mechanics and branching realities

Quantum mechanics, the part of physical science that arrangements with the way of behaving of particles at the nuclear and subatomic scale, has reliably tested our natural comprehension of the actual world. Among the many fascinating and in some cases bewildering parts of quantum mechanics, one of the most cryptic is the idea of expanding real factors, frequently connected with the Many-Universes Translation (MWI). This translation, first proposed by Hugh Everett III in 1957, recommends that with each quantum occasion having numerous potential results, the universe parts into a large number of equal real factors, each addressing an alternate result. In this investigation, we will dig into the center standards of quantum mechanics, the improvement of the Many-Universes Understanding, its suggestions, reactions, and the continuous discussions encompassing expanding real factors.

Quantum Mechanics: The Underpinning of The real world

Prior to diving into the complexities of the Many-Universes Translation, it's critical to lay out a primary comprehension of quantum mechanics, the structure whereupon this understanding is fabricated. Quantum mechanics, otherwise called quantum material science, quantum hypothesis, or wave mechanics, is a part of physical science that was created in the mid twentieth hundred years to make sense of the way of behaving of issue and energy at the littlest scales.

At the core of quantum mechanics lies the idea of wave-molecule duality, which recommends that particles like electrons and photons can display both molecule like and wave-like properties. This duality challenges the traditional, deterministic perspective on the world, where the way of behaving of particles is not entirely set in stone. In the quantum domain, particles don't have distinct properties until they are estimated, and their way of behaving is portrayed probabilistically.

The groundwork of quantum mechanics can be summed up through a few key standards:

Superposition: Quantum superposition is the idea that a quantum framework can exist in a blend of different states or positions all the while. This really intends that, for instance, an electron can exist in a superposition of various energy states, and a photon can all the while follow different ways through a twofold cut explore.

Quantization: In the quantum world, amounts like energy levels are quantized, meaning they come in discrete, particular qualities as opposed to a constant reach.

This is obvious in the quantized energy levels of electrons in particles and the quantization of precise force.

Likelihood and Vulnerability: Quantum mechanics is intrinsically probabilistic. Rather than having exact, unsurprising estimations, quantum hypothesis gives probabilities to different results. This probabilistic nature is portrayed by the wave capability, which addresses the likelihood dispersion of a molecule's potential states.

Wave Capability Breakdown: One of the focal conundrums in quantum mechanics is the breakdown of the wave capability upon estimation. The demonstration of estimation appears to "force" the quantum framework into one of its potential states, actually deleting the superposition. This idea is fundamental in grasping the Many-Universes Translation.

The Introduction of the Many-Universes Translation

The Many-Universes Translation (MWI) of quantum mechanics arose as an endeavor to address a portion of the key issues and oddities inside the hypothesis. The MWI was first proposed by Hugh Everett III in quite a while doctoral paper at Princeton College in 1957, named "Relative State Plan of Quantum Mechanics."

Everett's methodology was a takeoff from the overarching understandings of quantum mechanics, especially the Copenhagen translation, which was the predominant structure at that point. The Copenhagen translation, created by Niels Bohr and Werner Heisenberg, presented the idea of wave capability breakdown, where a quantum framework goes from a superposition of states to a solitary, unequivocal state upon estimation.

Everett's Many-Universes Translation, interestingly, dismissed the breakdown of the wave capability and proposed an alternate method for interpretting quantum mechanics. In the MWI, the wave capability never implodes, and all potential results of a quantum occasion are acknowledged in equal universes. Each time a quantum estimation is made, the universe parts into a huge number of equal real factors, each addressing one of the potential results.

The vital standards of the Many-Universes Translation include:

Fanning Universes: In the Many-Universes Understanding, each quantum occasion with numerous potential results prompts the formation of equal universes, frequently alluded to as "universes" or "branches." Each branch addresses an unmistakable result of the occasion.

Conjunction of Real factors: Significantly, the Many-Universes Understanding declares that this multitude of equal universes are similarly genuine. In every universe, the result of the quantum occasion is unmistakable, and the related the truth is as "genuine" as our own. This understanding difficulties the idea of a solitary, objective reality and recommends that numerous real factors coincide.

Deterministic Wave Capability Advancement: In the Many-Universes Translation, the development of the wave capability is represented by deterministic conditions, implying that the results in each branch are not still up in the air by the quantum regulations. This deterministic advancement is one of the key elements that recognize the MWI from different understandings.

The Many-Universes Understanding was earth shattering in a few regards:

Goal of the Estimation Issue: The MWI offered an answer for the estimation issue in quantum mechanics. Rather than conjuring the secretive and erratic breakdown of the wave capability upon estimation, the MWI proposes that the demonstration of estimation only decides the onlooker's state in a particular part of the universe, with all potential results acknowledged in equal branches.

End of the Requirement for Buried Factors: The MWI gave a method for interpretting quantum mechanics without the requirement for buried factors, which were hypothesized by certain translations, for example, the pilot-wave hypothesis. In the MWI, the wave capability contains all the data expected to portray the quantum framework.

Dismissal of the Copenhagen Understanding's Emotional Component: The Copenhagen translation presented the possibility that estimation includes an unchangeable abstract component. Conversely, the MWI portrays the demonstration of estimation as an actual cycle inside the quantum framework, taking out the requirement for emotional components in the understanding.

Ramifications of the Many-Universes Translation

The Many-Universes Translation has significant ramifications for how we might interpret quantum mechanics, the idea of the real world, and different areas of science and reasoning. How about we investigate a portion of the vital ramifications of the MWI:

Goal of the Estimation Issue: One of the focal difficulties in quantum mechanics is the estimation issue, which relates to the breakdown of the wave capability upon estimation. The MWI gives a rich answer for this issue by stating that the wave capability doesn't fall. All things considered, it keeps on developing, with every conceivable result prompting the production of another universe. This translation takes out the requirement for hypothesizing a different cycle for wave capability breakdown.

Determinism versus Indeterminism: The Many-Universes Understanding difficulties the conventional polarity among determinism and indeterminism in quantum mechanics. While it recognizes that quantum occasions are probabilistic and uncertain at the quantum level, it states that the development of the wave capability is deterministic. In this structure, each conceivable result is understood, and the advancement of the wave capability is represented by deterministic conditions.

Understanding of Quantum Trials: The Many-Universes Translation gives an alternate point of view on the results of quantum tests. It recommends that when an estimation is made, it isn't simply uncovering a previous reality yet deciding the result in the eyewitness' part of the universe. This has significant ramifications for the job of onlookers in quantum tests and the idea of quantum reality.

Quantum Trap: Quantum entrapment, a peculiarity where particles become connected so that the condition of one molecule is reliant upon the condition of another, is a major part of quantum mechanics. The Many-Universes Understanding offers a novel viewpoint on ensnarement. In this system, snared particles are not imparting across space promptly, as recommended by different translations, yet rather their states become related because of their common history in a similar part of the universe prior to expanding happens.

Quantum Figuring: The Many-Universes Translation has suggestions for quantum registering, a field that takes advantage of the standards of quantum mechanics to perform calculations at speeds unimaginable for traditional PCs.

Quantum PCs depend on the possibility of superposition, and the MWI gives a clever viewpoint on how quantum calculations work. In the idea of equal universes coinciding, quantum PCs can investigate numerous arrangements all the while, possibly altering the field of calculation.

Philosophical Ramifications: The Many-Universes Translation has significant philosophical ramifications. It challenges our conventional ideas of the real world, character, and independence. In a multiverse with expanding universes, the idea of "self" turns out to be more complicated, as each decision and result lead to the production of various variants of oneself. It prompts philosophical investigations into the idea of character, individual decisions, and the idea of self with regards to a multiverse.

2.3 Implications for the nature of reality

The Many-Universes Translation (MWI) of quantum mechanics, with its extreme idea of fanning real factors and equal universes, conveys significant ramifications for how we might interpret the idea of the real world. It challenges conventional originations of the real world, brings up issues about the job of eyewitnesses, and prompts philosophical investigations into the idea of presence, personality, and the actual universe. In this conversation, we will investigate the ramifications of the MWI for the idea of the real world, addressing philosophical, otherworldly, and epistemological parts of this notable translation.

1. **Multiverse and the Idea of The real world:**

   At the core of the Many-Universes Translation lies the thought of a multiverse, an immense outfit of equal real factors, each addressing an alternate result of quantum occasions. The presence of these fanning universes represents a basic test to our ordinary comprehension of the real world. In the traditional perspective, the truth is viewed as solitary, still up in the air. Nonetheless, the MWI recommends that numerous equal real factors coincide, each similarly genuine, leading to an in a general sense different origination of the real world.

   In the MWI, the truth isn't restricted to a solitary, fixed state yet is circulated across a limitless number of equal branches. This brings up issues about the idea of reality itself: Is reality solitary and goal, or is it, as the MWI proposes, a complex of coinciding potential outcomes? The idea of stretching real factors provokes us to reevaluate the actual embodiment of what comprises reality.

2. **The Job of Spectators in Quantum Reality:**
   One of the most captivating parts of the Many-Universes Understanding is its treatment of the job of spectators in quantum occasions. In conventional translations of quantum mechanics, the demonstration of estimation assumes a focal part, as it is accepted to fall the quantum wave capability and decide a solitary result. This emotional component in quantum mechanics has prompted conversations about the job of awareness in the breakdown of the wave capability.

   The MWI offers an alternate point of view. It sets that when a spectator makes an estimation, they become caught with the quantum framework being noticed, and their not entirely set in stone in one of the potential results. As such, the demonstration of estimation isn't making a solitary result happen but instead characterizing the eyewitness' state inside their separate part of the multiverse.

   This change in context brings up significant issues about the idea of cognizance, perception, and the job of onlookers in forming their world. Assuming the MWI is right, it suggests that spectators are personally associated with the quantum frameworks they measure and that their emotional not entirely settled by the specific branch they regard themselves as in. This viewpoint challenges traditional thoughts of objectivity and subjectivity with regards to quantum peculiarities.

3. **The Idea of Self and Personality:**
   The Many-Universes Translation presents an original perspective about private character and oneself. In a multiverse where stretching real factors happen with each quantum occasion, each decision, and each conceivable result, the idea of "self" turns out to be more perplexing. In the MWI, every decision you make brings about the formation of various variants of yourself in equal universes.

   This prompts captivating philosophical inquiries regarding the idea of personality. What's the significance here to be "you" in a multiverse where endless renditions of yourself exist, each carrying on with out various life ways and pursuing particular decisions? The MWI challenges the conventional thought of a particular and consistent self, provoking investigations into the idea of character and individual coherence.

   Scholars have investigated the possibility that our healthy identity is a composite of the multitude of renditions of ourselves across the multiverse. Each branch addresses an alternate feature of our character, and the amount of this multitude of features is the intricacy of our selfhood. This understanding opens up new points of view on the idea of oneself and the philosophical idea of individual personality.

4. **Relativity of Profound quality and Morals:**
   The MWI's suggestions reach out to the domain of morals and profound

quality. Equal universes, each containing various results of decisions and activities, brings up issues about the relativity of profound quality. In a multiverse, the results of our moral choices might fluctuate across various branches, and activities considered ethically off-base in one reality might prompt various results in another.

This prompts contemplations about the relativity of morals and the all inclusiveness of moral standards. Assuming the MWI is right, might there be a goal and generally material moral structure, or is profound quality dependent upon the particular part of reality in which one exists? The idea of fanning real factors provokes us to rethink the underpinnings of moral and moral way of thinking.

Also, spreading real factors conveys suggestions for the idea of moral obligation. In a multiverse, people might go with various decisions in various branches, prompting differing moral results. This brings up issues about whether people ought to be considered ethically answerable for activities that happen in parts of reality where they didn't go with those decisions deliberately. The MWI acquaints intricacies with the conventional comprehension of moral responsibility.

5. **Presence, all things considered:**
The Many-Universes Understanding affirms that all potential results of quantum occasions are acknowledged in equal universes. This suggests that each chance, regardless of how unrealistic or apparently fantastical, has its spot in the multiverse. The presence of all prospects difficulties our instincts about what is possible or incomprehensible.

In the MWI, there is a universe wherein you settled on each possible decision, regardless of how disconnected or improbable it might appear. For instance, there is a universe wherein you turned into an incredibly famous craftsman, and one more in which you sought after a profession as a space explorer. The presence of these different conceivable outcomes challenges how we might interpret the imperatives of the real world and the constraints of what can be understood.

The possibility that each conceivable result exists in the multiverse prompts inquiries concerning the idea of probability and potential. Does the presence of these horde prospects recommend that human potential is boundless, compelled exclusively by the decisions one makes in a specific part of the multiverse? The idea of spreading real factors urges us to investigate the limits of plausibility and rethink what we consider reachable.

6. **The Enormous Viewpoint:**
The Many-Universes Translation broadens its suggestions past the quantum domain and into the enormous point of view. Assuming each quantum occasion prompts spreading real factors, this infers that the whole universe is penetrated by a tremendous, interconnected organization of equal universes. The scale and extent of the multiverse challenge our origination of the universe.

From a grandiose outlook, the MWI proposes that the universe is certainly not a solitary, separated substance yet is important for a more extensive multiverse, with multitudinous real factors unfurling in equal. This point of view brings up issues about the interconnectedness of these equal universes and the idea of inestimable presence. How do these fanning real factors connect with the more extensive universe, and what does this infer for how we might interpret the universe in general?

Also, the idea of fanning real factors conveys suggestions for the quest for extra-terrestrial life and the chance of developments in equal universes. The MWI recommends that some place in the multiverse, different types of life might exist, each with its own novel history and advancement. This thought extends the extent of astrobiology and the quest for life in the universe.

7. **Epistemological Difficulties:**

The Many-Universes Translation presents significant epistemological difficulties, especially with regards to logical information and the idea of truth. In a multiverse where all potential results are understood, it becomes muddled how we can decide the reality of a specific assertion or speculation.

For instance, in a universe where a logical examination produces one outcome and in another universe, it yields an alternate outcome, which result is "reality"? This brings up issues about the idea of logical information and the relativity of truth in a multiverse. It prompts us to reexamine how we characterize logical objectivity and truth in a reality where all prospects exist.

The MWI additionally challenges how we might interpret information and proof. In a multiverse, what considers proof, and how would we lay out the legitimacy of a specific logical hypothesis or speculation? The presence of equal real factors difficulties our ordinary ideas of observational confirmation and the dependability of logical request.

8. **Moral and Commonsense Contemplations:**

Equal universes raises moral and commonsense contemplations. On the off chance that each conceivable result is acknowledged in an alternate part of the multiverse, what moral contemplations ought to direct our activities in the current reality? Do our decisions in a single part of reality have moral ramifications for different branches, regardless of whether those branches exist past our immediate mindfulness?

Moreover, the idea of stretching real factors might have suggestions for independent direction and individual options. Assuming each decision we make brings about the formation of various variants of ourselves in the multiverse, how does this influence our way to deal with navigation and the outcomes of our activities? The MWI prompts us to ponder the expected importance and repercussions of our decisions in a more extensive setting.

9. **Cosmological Importance:**
The Many-Universes Understanding stretches out its suggestions to the universe all in all. In the event that the multiverse exists, it brings up issues about the beginning and nature of the multiverse itself. What cycles or instruments could prompt the formation of a limitless number of stretching real factors? This has suggestions for cosmology and our comprehension of the basic idea of the universe.

Furthermore, the idea of expanding real factors prompts investigations into the astronomical meaning of humankind and the Earth. In a multiverse with endless conceivable outcomes, the presence of Earth and human existence might be one of numerous likely results. This point of view difficulties our customary human-centric perspective on the universe and urges us to investigate the more extensive astronomical setting where our reality unfurls.

10. **Interconnectedness of Real factors:**

The Many-Universes Translation recommends that all equal universes are interconnected through the quantum ensnarement of particles and the common history of quantum frameworks prior to fanning happens. This interconnectedness challenges how we might interpret the detachment and separateness of real factors. In a multiverse, there is a feeling of enormous solidarity and reliance among all branches.

The interconnectedness of real factors additionally brings up issues about the potential for correspondence or collaboration between equal universes. While the MWI doesn't propose direct contact between branches, it prompts hypothesis about the chance of sharing data or encounters across various real factors. This thought has enlivened sci-fi and creative investigations of interdimensional correspondence.

Taking everything into account, the Many-Universes Translation of quantum mechanics conveys significant ramifications for how we might interpret the idea of the real world, awareness, morals, and the universe. The idea of spreading real factors difficulties our conventional ideas of the real world and prompts philosophical investigations into the idea of self, character, and the moral outcomes of our activities. The possibility of an interconnected multiverse has suggestions for how we might interpret the universe, the interconnectedness of real factors, and the potential for enormous importance. While the MWI stays a subject of discussion and investigation, it fills in as a provocative system for reconsidering the idea of reality with regards to quantum mechanics and the multiverse. As how we might interpret quantum mechanics and the idea of spreading real factors develops, we might keep on revealing new experiences into the significant ramifications of this translation for our view of the real world and presence.

Chapter 3

Quantum Entanglement and Parallel Realities

Quantum ensnarement and equal truths are two of the most charming and complex ideas in current physical science. They challenge how we might interpret the essential idea of the universe and can possibly upset our view of the real world. In this investigation, we will dive into the significant thoughts behind these peculiarities and how they are interconnected, despite the fact that they have a place with various parts of physical science.

Quantum entrapment, frequently portrayed as "creepy activity a ways off" by Albert Einstein, alludes to the puzzling and non-nearby association between at least two particles. This association challenges old style instincts and recommends that the properties of these particles are snared so that an adjustment of one molecule quickly influences the other, no matter what the actual distance that isolates them. This peculiarity was first hypothesized by Erwin Schrödinger in 1935, and it has since become one of the focal fundamentals of quantum mechanics.

To embrace the idea of quantum trap, one should grasp the essentials of quantum mechanics. At the core of this hypothesis is the wave capability, a numerical portrayal of a molecule's state. The wave capability contains all the data about a molecule, including its situation, force, and other perceptible properties. At the point when two particles become entrapped, their wave capabilities become corresponded so that any adjustment of one molecule's wave capability quickly influences the other's, regardless of how far separated they are. This immediate association between caught particles has been tentatively noticed and checked on many times, prompting the end that quantum snare is an inborn component of the quantum world.

One of the most well known tests representing quantum entrapment is the Einstein-Podolsky-Rosen (EPR) analyze. In this examination, two particles are ready in a state where their properties, like twist, are corresponded. At the point when one of the particles is estimated, the estimation result in a split second decides the result of the estimation for the other molecule, no matter what the division between them.

This peculiarity has bewildered physicists for quite a long time and stays one of the most baffling parts of quantum physical science.

While quantum ensnarement is a deep rooted peculiarity, its suggestions for how we might interpret the universe are as yet a subject of discussion. A few physicists view snare as proof of non-territory, recommending that data can be communicated quicker than the speed of light. Notwithstanding, this translation brings up critical issues about causality and the design of spacetime. Others contend that quantum snare isn't an infringement of the standard of territory yet rather an impression of the interconnectedness of the quantum world, where particles can exist in superposition states and are not restricted by traditional limits.

One of the most charming parts of quantum entrapment is its true capacity for down to earth applications. Snared particles can be outfit for quantum correspondence, for example, quantum key dissemination, which offers extraordinary security in information transmission. Quantum PCs, which influence the exceptional properties of trapped particles, hold the commitment of taking care of intricate issues definitely more effectively than old style PCs. These applications show that quantum entrapment isn't only a hypothetical interest however a peculiarity with genuine ramifications.

Presently, let us shift our concentration to the idea of equal real factors. While quantum trap manages the way of behaving of particles at the quantum level, equal real factors or resemble universes propose the presence of various, unmistakable universes that coincide close by our own. This thought is established in the understanding of quantum mechanics known as the Many-Universes Translation (MWI), first figured out by Hugh Everett III during the 1950s.

As per the MWI, at whatever point a quantum occasion happens, all potential results really occur, however they occur in discrete parts of the real world. At the end of the day, if you somehow happened to notice a quantum molecule's twist, for instance, in one universe, it very well may turn clockwise, while in another universe, it very well may turn counterclockwise. This translation recommends that there are incalculable equal real factors, each expanding from a quantum occasion, making a limitless multiverse.

The idea of equal real factors difficulties our traditional comprehension of the real world and brings up significant issues about the idea of presence and oneself. In the event that the Many-Universes Translation is right, every choice, regardless of how trifling, would prompt the making of another universe. This suggests that there are boundless variants of ourselves, each carrying on with various lives and pursuing various decisions in endless equal real factors.

Equal real factors has enamored the creative mind of sci-fi creators and scholars the same. It has been investigated in writing, film, and TV, where characters frequently cross between equal universes, experiencing substitute adaptations of themselves and the world. While these imaginary depictions might appear to be unrealistic, they draw motivation from the significant and confounding ramifications of the Many-Universes Understanding.

The association between quantum trap and equal real factors may not be quickly self-evident, yet a few physicists have proposed charming connections between the two ideas. One speculation proposes that the non-nearby associations made by ensnared particles could be a consequence of collaborations between various parts of reality in the multiverse. In this view, ensnared particles are not conveying across space yet rather across various universes.

Moreover, a few physicists have guessed that the demonstration of perception and estimation in quantum material science might be liable for the fanning of equal real factors. As per this understanding, when we measure a quantum framework, we are not only uncovering the properties of that framework; we are likewise choosing a specific part of reality wherein those properties exist. This suggests that our perceptions are personally associated with the production of equal universes, adding a philosophical aspect to the demonstration of estimation in quantum mechanics.

It's vital for note that the Many-Universes Translation is only one of a few understandings of quantum mechanics, and it stays a subject of progressing discussion and exploration inside the material science local area. While the MWI gives a convincing system to understanding quantum peculiarities and equal real factors, it isn't the main translation, and different understandings, for example, the Copenhagen translation or the pilot-wave hypothesis, offer elective points of view on the idea of quantum reality.

The investigation of quantum snare and equal real factors opens a door to significant philosophical and supernatural inquiries. One such inquiry is the idea of awareness and its job in molding reality. On the off chance that each perception and estimation prompts the formation of another part of the real world, does cognizance assume a key part in the construction of the multiverse? This thought has started banters about the idea of awareness, choice, and the connection between the eyewitness and the saw in the quantum world.

In addition, the presence of equal real factors difficulties how we might interpret causality and determinism. In a multiverse where all potential results happen, does the idea of circumstances and logical results lose its importance? Are occasions foreordained, or do they emerge from decisions in various parts of the real world? These inquiries have significant ramifications for how we might interpret time and the idea of the universe.

The idea of equal real factors additionally brings up issues about the potential for correspondence or collaboration between various parts of the real world. Assuming that equal universes exist, is it conceivable to access or impact them? A few speculative hypotheses propose that specific peculiarities, for example, a sensation that this has happened before or precognition, might be looks into equal real factors or the capacity to take advantage of data from different parts of the multiverse. Be that as it may, these thoughts remain profoundly speculative and need observational proof.

In the domain of quantum ensnarement, the association between particles, paying little mind to remove, challenges how we might interpret existence. It indicates the chance of non-territory, where data can be communicated immediately, apparently disregarding the speed of light's vast speed limit. While this idea is confusing, it likewise has commonsense ramifications for quantum correspondence and processing. Quantum ensnarement frames the reason for quantum instant transportation, a cycle by which the quantum condition of one molecule can be sent to another, possibly empowering secure and quick correspondence over tremendous distances.

Quantum figuring, another region where entrapment assumes a urgent part, offers the possibility to tackle issues that are right now unmanageable for traditional PCs. Quantum PCs influence the force of superposition and entrapment to effectively perform complex estimations more. This has extensive applications in fields like cryptography, material science, and improvement issues, with the possibility to upset ventures and logical examination.

The connection between quantum entrapment and equal real factors might appear to be speculative, yet it mirrors the continuous mission to grasp the real essence of the quantum world. A few physicists and specialists keep on investigating the associations between these two ideas, looking to overcome any barrier between quantum mechanics and the presence of a multiverse. While no decisive proof backings such associations, the tempting prospects they present rouse further examination and hypothetical investigation.

3.1 Understanding quantum entanglement

Understanding quantum snare is fundamental for grasping quite possibly of the most confounding and baffling peculiarity in the domain of material science. This peculiarity, frequently depicted as "creepy activity a ways off" by Albert Einstein, is a key part of quantum mechanics, and it challenges our old style instincts about the way of behaving of particles. In this investigation, we will dive profound into the complexities of quantum trap, looking at its verifiable turn of events, fundamental standards, trial proof, and possible ramifications.

The idea of quantum snare arose in the mid twentieth 100 years because of the progressive improvements in quantum mechanics. It addresses a basic takeoff from old style material science and presents the idea that particles can become interconnected in a way that resists our traditional comprehension of actual reality. The groundwork of quantum trap lies in the standards of superposition and quantum states.

Superposition is a central idea in quantum mechanics that portrays the capacity of quantum frameworks to at the same time exist in different states. In the old style world, an item is in a solitary, positive state at some random time. For instance, a light switch can be either on or off, yet not both on the double. Conversely, quantum frameworks can exist in a superposition of states. For example, an electron can all the while exist in numerous positions, or a photon can be in a superposition of polarizations. This intrinsic property of quantum frameworks is vital to grasping trap.

Quantum states are numerical depictions of the properties and qualities of a quantum framework. These states are addressed by a numerical develop called a wave capability, which embodies all the data about a quantum framework's properties, like position, force, twist, or polarization. Quantum states are regularly communicated as vectors in a complicated vector space, utilizing numerical formalism that is fundamental for grasping entrapment.

To comprehend quantum ensnarement, we want to consider a situation including at least two particles. These particles can be electrons, photons, or some other quantum substances. At the point when two particles communicate such that outcomes in their quantum states becoming corresponded, they are supposed to be trapped. This relationship implies that the quantum properties of one molecule are naturally associated with the properties of the other, regardless of whether they are isolated by huge distances. This interconnectedness separates quantum trap from traditional material science.

The historical backdrop of quantum ensnarement is entwined with the improvement of quantum mechanics itself. In 1935, the Austrian physicist Erwin Schrödinger presented the expression "snare" while portraying a psychological study that would become perhaps of the most renowned oddity throughout the entire existence of material science — the Schrödinger's feline Catch 22. This psychological test was intended to show the strange idea of quantum superposition and snare.

In the Schrödinger's feline Catch 22, a feline is set in a fixed box with a radioactive iota, a Geiger counter, a vial of toxic substance, and a radioactive source. On the off chance that the Geiger counter recognizes radiation, it sets off the arrival of the toxic substance, bringing about the feline's demise. Be that as it may, on the off chance that no radiation is distinguished, the feline remaining parts alive. As per quantum mechanics, until the container is opened and the feline is noticed, it exists in a superposition of states, both alive and dead at the same time.

This conundrum features that particles, like the radioactive molecule and the feline, can exist in superpositions until noticed. The demonstration of perception or estimation, in quantum mechanics, implodes the superposition and powers the framework into one of its potential states. On account of the feline, it stays in a superposition of both alive and dead until the container is opened, and its still up in the air through perception.

While Schrödinger's feline is a psychological study and not a genuine actual framework, it effectively outlines the unusual and unreasonable nature of quantum mechanics. It shows the way that in the quantum world, particles can be caught in superpositions of states, and the demonstration of perception assumes a urgent part in deciding their properties.

The EPR Catch 22 and the Introduction of Quantum Trap

The idea of quantum entrapment got huge consideration in the last part of the 1920s and mid 1930s, principally because of crafted by Albert Einstein, Boris

Podolsky, and Nathan Rosen, aggregately known as EPR. In 1935, they distributed a fundamental paper, frequently alluded to as the EPR paper, which presented the idea of trap and brought up basic issues about the fulfillment and ramifications of quantum mechanics.

The EPR paper zeroed in on a specific kind of snare including properties like position and force. It proposed a psychological study that thought about two ensnared particles, like electrons, with known, corresponding properties. As indicated by the standards of quantum mechanics, in the event that the place of one molecule is exactly known, its force becomes questionable, as well as the other way around.

The EPR psychological test, generally, found out if the quantum depiction of snared particles gave a total image of the particles' properties or on the other hand assuming there were covered up factors — unseen properties or data — that would represent their way of behaving without disregarding the standards of traditional material science. EPR's contention was a test to the probabilistic, indeterministic nature of quantum mechanics and looked to show that it prompted a deficient portrayal of the real world.

Einstein broadly communicated his uneasiness with the probabilistic idea of quantum mechanics by saying, "God doesn't play dice with the universe." He accepted that there ought to be covered up factors that decided the results of quantum estimations, and the clear indeterminacy of quantum mechanics was a consequence of our absence of information about these factors.

Be that as it may, in 1964, the physicist John Chime planned a progression of disparities, known as Ringer's imbalances, which could be tried through tests. Chime's work showed that any hypothesis in light of stowed away factors should fulfill specific circumstances, and assuming these circumstances were disregarded, it would suggest that quantum mechanics is non-neighborhood — data can be communicated momentarily over tremendous distances. This would straightforwardly challenge the standards of traditional material science and the thought of region, which Einstein had unequivocally upheld.

Tests Testing Quantum Snare

Ringer's imbalances laid the foundation for exploratory trial of quantum snare. Throughout the long term, various investigations have been directed to test the expectations of quantum mechanics and decide if trapped particles show conduct that is predictable with the hypothesis.

One of the earliest examinations to test Ringer's imbalances was led by physicist John Clauser during the 1970s. Clauser's investigation, frequently alluded to as the Clauser-Horne try, serious areas of strength for gave against neighborhood stowed away factors. Resulting tests by Alain Angle during the 1980s further affirmed the infringement of Ringer's disparities, offering undeniable proof that quantum entrapment prompts non-neighborhood relationships between's particles.

The infringement of Chime's disparities showed that quantum trap brings about relationships between's ensnared particles that can't be made sense of by old style physical science. It suggests that the properties of these particles are interconnected in a manner that rises above traditional limits and difficulties the guideline of region, which specifies that data can't be sent quicker than the speed of light.

One of the most popular trials outlining quantum snare is the Angle try. In this trial, a couple of trapped photons is delivered and isolated over significant distances. At the point when estimations are made on these photons, their properties are viewed as corresponded, despite the fact that they are far separated. These relationships happen quickly, proposing that data is sent between the ensnared photons quicker than the speed of light, which is an immediate infringement of traditional material science.

The Angle analyze, alongside other comparable analyses, areas of strength for gave for non-territory and quantum snare. It exhibited that snared particles share a strange and prompt association that challenges old style clarifications.

Quantum Trap and the Ringer Hypothesis

Chime's hypothesis, which is gotten from Ringer's imbalances, significantly affects the field of quantum physical science. The hypothesis demonstrates that no hypothesis in light of neighborhood stowed away factors can imitate the factual expectations of quantum mechanics, and the noticed relationships between's snared particles should be non-nearby.

The ramifications of Ringer's hypothesis are significant. They propose that the idea of region, a major precept of traditional material science, doesn't hold at the quantum level. All things considered, quantum ensnarement presents a type of quick, non-nearby association between particles, a peculiarity broadly depicted by Einstein as "creepy activity a ways off."

While the trials that test Chime's disparities support the expectations of quantum mechanics and the non-neighborhood nature of quantum entrapment, they don't give a system to make sense of how entrapped particles impart quickly.

This stays one of the persevering through secrets of quantum entrapment and a subject of progressing exploration and discussion inside established researchers.

3.2 Theories of entanglement connecting parallel worlds

Interfacing quantum trap with equal universes or equal universes is an idea that has interested physicists and caught the creative mind of the general population. While this idea is still to a great extent speculative and falls into the domain of hypothetical material science, it can possibly reshape how we might interpret the universe and reality itself. In this investigation, we will dive into the different speculations and theories that look to lay out an association between quantum entrapment and equal universes.

Many-Universes Translation (MWI): The Many-Universes Understanding, presented by Hugh Everett III during the 1950s, is quite possibly of the most notable hypothesis that associates quantum trap to the presence of equal universes. As per the MWI, each time a quantum occasion happens, all potential results really occur, however they happen in discrete, non-conveying parts of the real world. As such, when a quantum framework exists in a superposition of states, the universe parts into numerous branches, each comparing to an alternate conceivable result.

This understanding recommends that quantum trap, which includes the superposition of states for caught particles, prompts the making of equal real factors. At the point when an estimation is made on an entrapped framework, the universe bifurcates into branches, with each branch relating to an alternate estimation result. This suggests that the relationships saw in trap tests are a consequence of communications between various parts of the real world.

The Many-Universes Translation is an extreme takeoff from old style instincts and offers a special point of view on the idea of quantum reality. It proposes a multiverse where all conceivable quantum results happen, and each branch addresses an alternate rendition of the real world. While the MWI is an exceptionally discussed and dubious understanding, it stays a convincing hypothesis that interfaces quantum trap with the presence of equal universes.

The Conditional Translation of Quantum Mechanics: The Value-based Understanding, proposed by John G. Cramer, offers an elective clarification for quantum ensnarement and its association with equal universes. In this understanding, quantum cooperations are considered to be a "exchange" between cutting edge (future) and hindered (past) waves.

With regards to snare, when two particles become caught, they trade progressed and hindered waves that convey data about their properties. These waves travel in reverse and forward in time, making an exchange that interfaces the two particles. As per the Value-based Understanding, the high level waves relate to the ensnared accomplice's wave capability, and the exchange brings about the noticed relationships between's snared particles.

According to the point of view of this translation, the association between entrapped particles isn't really characteristic of equal universes yet rather a remarkable approach to grasping quantum communications. Notwithstanding, a few translations of the Conditional Understanding recommend that the exchange cycle might include communications with different parts of the real world, indicating an association with equal universes.

Bohmian Mechanics and the Pilot-Wave Hypothesis: Bohmian Mechanics, otherwise called the pilot-wave hypothesis, offers an alternate way to deal with quantum trap that includes the possibility of a secret variable hypothesis. In this understanding, particles have clear cut positions and directions, yet they are directed by a secret pilot wave that decides their way of behaving. At the point when two particles become trapped, their pilot waves are corresponded, bringing about the noticed non-neighborhood connections.

While Bohmian Mechanics itself doesn't innately associate trap to resemble universes, it has roused elective understandings that in all actuality do investigate this thought. A few physicists have recommended that the pilot waves might reach out into equal real factors, proposing that entrapped particles are associated with different parts of the multiverse. This expansion of the pilot waves into equal universes raises charming opportunities for figuring out the idea of ensnarement.

Quantum Nonlocality and Superdeterminism: A hypotheses that endeavor to interface quantum trap with equal universes summon the idea of superdeterminism. Superdeterminism places that all occasions in the universe are interconnected and foreordained all along, intending that there is no obvious irregularity or unrestrained choice. In such a system, the clear non-nearby relationships saw in entrapment tests are not a consequence of particles conveying across space or through equal universes however are rather a result of foreordained, interconnected occasions.

While superdeterminism is an exceptionally disputable and revolutionary thought, it challenges the traditional comprehension of ensnarement and causality. It recommends that the relationships between's entrapped particles are an indication of a more profound, foreordained reality, where each occasion is associated across existence. This understanding doesn't require the presence of equal universes, however it questions the underpinnings of quantum mechanics and the idea of trap.

It's vital to underscore that the association between quantum trap and equal universes remains profoundly speculative and has not been convincingly settled through experimental proof. These hypotheses and translations are still subjects of progressing examination and discussion inside mainstream researchers. They address endeavors to accommodate the weird and strange peculiarities of quantum mechanics with how we might interpret reality, yet they likewise bring up significant philosophical issues about the idea of the universe.

One of the vital difficulties in investigating the association among entrapment and equal universes is the trouble of testing and confirming these speculations. Large numbers of the proposed hypotheses include parts of quantum mechanics that are at present past the extent of our trial capacities. Moreover, the idea of equal universes, assuming that they exist, might be innately out of reach to us, making direct observational affirmation testing.

Regardless of the speculative idea of these hypotheses, they proceed to move and drive research in the field of quantum physical science. They challenge how we might interpret reality, causality, and the design of the universe, pushing the limits of our insight and inciting us to reexamine the essential standards of material science.

3.3 Experimental evidence and ongoing research

Trial proof and progressing research in the domain of quantum entrapment assume a vital part in our mission to figure out this secretive peculiarity. Throughout the long term, researchers have directed a large number of examinations pointed toward testing the expectations of quantum mechanics and looking at the properties of ensnared particles. These investigations not just offer help for the legitimacy of quantum ensnarement yet additionally open up new roads for investigating the possible applications and ramifications of this peculiarity.

To see the value in the meaning of trial proof in the investigation of quantum ensnarement, we should initially recognize that entrapment is a crucial part of quantum mechanics. A peculiarity opposes old style instincts and difficulties how we might interpret the idea of the universe. One of the main attributes of trap is the quick relationship of properties between ensnared particles, no matter what the actual division between them.

In the beginning of quantum mechanics, this non-nearby part of snare was a subject of discussion and concern. Albert Einstein, Boris Podolsky, and Nathan Rosen, by and large known as EPR, broadly distributed a paper in 1935 that brought up issues about the fulfillment of quantum mechanics and the idea of trap. They proposed a psychological study that meant to show the innate non-territory of ensnared particles and addressed whether the hypothesis gave a total portrayal of actual reality.

Einstein, specifically, was upset by the possibility that caught particles could impact each other immediately, apparently disregarding the standard of territory, which expresses that no data can be sent quicker than the speed of light. This prompted the renowned declaration that quantum ensnarement included "creepy activity a good ways off."

Be that as it may, as quantum mechanics created and exploratory strategies progressed, researchers started to test the forecasts of the hypothesis and look at the idea of snare all the more intently. One of the main commitments to this field was crafted by physicist John Chime, who formed a progression of disparities known as Ringer's imbalances.

Ringer's imbalances gave a structure to testing the expectations of quantum mechanics and deciding if snared particles displayed conduct reliable with traditional material science or whether they for sure exhibited non-nearby relationships. Chime's work laid out an establishment for trial examinations concerning quantum snare and the expected infringement of traditional limits.

Since the definition of Chime's disparities, various trials have been led to test these forecasts and investigate the properties of entrapped particles. The aftereffects of these examinations have given undeniable proof for quantum ensnarement and its non-neighborhood nature.

One of the earliest trials intended to test Chime's imbalances was directed by physicist John Clauser during the 1970s. Clauser's analysis, frequently alluded to as the Clauser-Horne explore, involved estimations on caught photons. The consequences of the analysis unequivocally abused the expectations of old style physical science, giving solid proof to the non-nearby nature of quantum ensnarement.

Ensuing tests by physicist Alain Viewpoint during the 1980s further affirmed the infringement of Chime's imbalances and supported the end that quantum trap prompts non-nearby relationships between's particles. Viewpoint's work was weighty, as it included estimating caught particles isolated by huge distances, as much as a few kilometers. The noticed relationships happened momentarily, recommending that data was being sent between the ensnared particles quicker than the speed of light.

The examinations directed by Perspective and others assumed a urgent part in laying out the trial proof for the non-region of quantum trap. These outcomes tested the traditional rule of territory and offered solid help for the expectations of quantum mechanics.

One of the most popular investigations delineating quantum trap is the Viewpoint analyze. In this trial, a couple of snared photons is delivered and isolated over significant distances. At the point when estimations are made on these photons, their properties are viewed as connected, despite the fact that they are far separated. These relationships happen immediately, recommending that data is communicated between the snared photons quicker than the speed of light, which is an immediate infringement of old style physical science.

The Perspective analysis, alongside other comparative examinations, gave solid proof for non-area and quantum snare. It exhibited that caught particles share a secretive and prompt association that resists old style clarifications.

The exploratory proof supporting quantum entrapment has sweeping ramifications for how we might interpret the universe and the possible utilizations of this peculiarity. While it is critical to perceive the significant meaning of these tests, recognizing the continuous examination and investigation in the field of quantum entanglement is similarly urgent.

One of the critical parts of progressing research in quantum trap is the improvement of new trial methods and advances. Propels in regions, for example, quantum optics, quantum data handling, and quantum processing have empowered researchers to direct more modern examinations and investigate the properties of entrapped particles with more prominent accuracy.

Quantum snare has viable applications in different fields, including quantum correspondence and quantum figuring. Quantum key dissemination, for instance, use the interesting properties of snared particles to make exceptionally secure correspondence frameworks. It takes into account the trading of encryption keys that are practically invulnerable to listening in, as any endeavor to catch the key would disturb the entrapped state and become promptly perceivable.

In the domain of quantum figuring, snare is a principal asset for performing complex computations more proficiently than old style PCs. Quantum PCs can use superposition and entrapment to handle data in manners that traditional PCs can't. This can possibly alter ventures and logical exploration in regions like cryptography, material science, and advancement issues.

Progressing research in quantum entrapment likewise investigates the essential idea of ensnared states and their suggestions for the construction of spacetime. A few physicists examine the connection among snare and the texture of the universe, intending to reveal the more profound associations between quantum mechanics and the calculation of spacetime.

Besides, there is continuous investigation of the job of trap in central inquiries concerning the idea of the real world, cognizance, and the spectator's effect on quantum frameworks. A few scientists dig into the philosophical and mystical components of entrapment, looking at how it challenges how we might interpret causality, determinism, and the job of the onlooker in molding quantum reality.

The idea of trap likewise assumes a focal part in the investigation of quantum snare and dark openings. The "dark opening data mystery" is a well established issue in material science, which questions whether data about particles that fall into a dark opening is lost until the end of time. A few physicists propose that snare could give an answer for this Catch 22 by permitting data to be encoded in caught particles on the outer layer of a dark opening.

Moreover, progressing research investigates the potential for bridling quantum snare for quantum instant transportation. Quantum instant transportation is a cycle that empowers the exchange of the quantum condition of one molecule to another, regardless of the actual distance between them. This has suggestions for secure correspondence and the improvement of cutting edge quantum organizations.

While trial proof has proactively exhibited the presence of quantum entrapment and its non-neighborhood properties, progressing research keeps on growing comprehension we might interpret this peculiarity and reveal new applications and suggestions. The investigation of quantum snare isn't restricted to the research facility yet stretches out to the domains of reasoning, power, and the actual texture of the actual universe.

In outline, trial proof has laid out the truth of quantum trap and its non-neighborhood nature, testing old style instincts and reshaping how we might interpret the actual world. Continuous examination in this field keeps on pushing the limits of our insight and investigate the significant ramifications of snare. From useful applications in quantum correspondence and processing to its job in central inquiries concerning the idea of the real world, quantum entrapment stays an entrancing and perplexing part of the universe that welcomes further examination and thought.

Chapter 4

Cosmic Microwave Background Radiation

Infinite Microwave Foundation Radiation (CMB), frequently alluded to as the glimmer of the Huge explosion, is a basic and interesting part of how we might interpret the universe. This weak, almost uniform radiation pervading the universe gives a preview of the universe's initial state and has significant ramifications for cosmology, astronomy, and our comprehension of the universe's starting points.

The account of CMB starts with the Theory of how things came to be, which is the predominant cosmological model that portrays the beginning of the universe. As indicated by this hypothesis, the universe began from an inconceivably hot, thick state around 13.8 quite a while back. As the universe extended, it cooled, and the main iotas, for the most part hydrogen and helium, shaped. The universe progressed from a condition of outrageous radiation control to one where matter, as iotas, turned into the prevailing part.

During the beginning phases of the universe, when it was still very hot and thick, photons, the particles of light, were caught in a high-energy plasma of charged particles. These photons oftentimes collaborated with charged particles, like electrons and protons, dispersing every which way. This extraordinary climate kept the photons from voyaging openly and made a "haze" that clouded our perspective on the universe's beginning phases.

Notwithstanding, as the universe proceeded to grow and cool, a crucial point in time happened roughly 380,000 years after the Huge explosion. Right now, the universe had cooled adequately for electrons to consolidate with protons, framing impartial hydrogen molecules. This interaction, known as recombination, significantly affected the universe's radiation. With the development of unbiased particles, the universe became straightforward to radiation.

As the universe progressed from a plasma of charged particles to a nonpartisan gas, the photons that were recently caught were out of nowhere allowed to go through space unrestricted. These photons, delivered during recombination, address the Vast

Microwave Foundation Radiation. They have been going through the universe for almost 13.8 billion years, contacting us today as a weak shine of microwave radiation.

The revelation of CMB is quite possibly of the most critical and celebrated accomplishment in the field of astronomy and cosmology. It was first distinguished by Arno Penzias and Robert Wilson in 1964, who were cosmologists at the Chime Phone Research centers in New Jersey. They were working with a huge, profoundly delicate microwave recieving wire and saw an unexplained foundation commotion that persevered in their perceptions.

Subsequent to directing careful examinations and precluding possible wellsprings of obstruction, for example, pigeon droppings or failing hardware, Penzias and Wilson understood that they had unintentionally found the Infinite Microwave Foundation Radiation. This disclosure gave undeniable proof on the side of the Theory of the universe's origin and denoted a huge achievement in how we might interpret the universe's initial history.

The presence of CMB is a basic piece of proof for the Theory of prehistoric cosmic detonation. It is frequently alluded to as the "conclusive evidence" of the Huge explosion since it validates the forecast that the universe was once in a hot, thick state and has been growing and cooling from that point onward.

CMB has a few fundamental qualities that make it a critical part of how we might interpret the universe:

Consistency: CMB is strikingly uniform, with almost a similar temperature saw this way and that. This consistency infers that the early universe was profoundly homogeneous, which is reliable with the forecasts of the Theory of how things came to be.

Blackbody Range: The range of CMB intently looks like that of a blackbody radiator. This phantom dispersion is one of the most reliable blackbody spectra at any point noticed and fills in as strong proof for the Theory of how things came to be.

Anisotropies: While CMB is exceptionally uniform, it additionally shows slight temperature varieties, known as anisotropies. These varieties are unquestionably little, regularly on the request for one section in 100,000, however they are of extraordinary importance in figuring out the development of designs in the universe.

The investigation of these anisotropies in CMB has given fundamental experiences into the arrangement of enormous designs, for example, universes and cosmic system bunches. These little temperature vacillations act as the seeds from which enormous designs developed through gravitational fascination. Subsequently, the vast microwave foundation is a fundamental instrument for figuring out the huge scope construction of the universe.

One of the most popular trials pointed toward planning the anisotropies in the CMB is the Wilkinson Microwave Anisotropy Test (WMAP). Sent off in 2001, the WMAP satellite studied the CMB with wonderful accuracy and created a point by point guide of the temperature varieties in the radiation. The information gathered by

WMAP has altogether worked on how we might interpret the universe's organization, age, and design.

Notwithstanding the WMAP mission, the European Space Organization's Planck satellite, sent off in 2009, made exact estimations of the CMB anisotropies, further refining how we might interpret the universe's properties. The Planck information has given bits of knowledge into the dissemination of issue, dull matter, and dim energy in the universe, revealing insight into the huge scope construction and development of the universe.

The anisotropies in the CMB are not just significant for grasping the arrangement of designs in the universe yet additionally for examining the underlying states of the universe. They offer important imperatives on the universe's boundaries and its sythesis, prompting key experiences into the idea of dull matter and dim energy, which together make up by far most of the universe's substance.

CMB anisotropies likewise support the hypothesis of vast expansion, which sets that the universe went through a fast and outstanding development at the times following the Huge explosion. Inflationary models foresee the presence of explicit examples in the CMB anisotropies, for example, slight deviations from wonderful isotropy and temperature vacillations that follow a particular factual circulation. Perceptions of these examples adjust well to inflationary expectations and loan backing to the inflationary model of the universe's initial development.

The point by point estimations of the grandiose microwave foundation radiation have prompted surprising advances in how we might interpret the universe's age, arrangement, and construction. They have offered fundamental help for the Theory of prehistoric cosmic detonation and have prompted the advancement of the Lambda-CDM model, which depicts the universe as comprising of dim matter, dull energy, and standard matter (like molecules).

One of the main discoveries from the investigation of CMB anisotropies is the assurance of the universe's age with phenomenal accuracy. The age of the universe, as determined from CMB information, is around 13.8 billion years. This worth lines up with other cosmological perceptions, for example, estimations of the Hubble steady, which decides the pace of the universe's development. The wonderful consistency of these autonomous estimations supports the vigor of how we might interpret infinite development.

Notwithstanding its part in deciding the universe's age, the examination of CMB information has given experiences into the universe's creation. It has uncovered that most of the universe's substance is as dull energy, a strange and unpleasant power liable for the sped up extension of the universe. Dull matter, which doesn't connect with light or different types of electromagnetic radiation, makes up a critical part of the universe's matter substance.

The rest of the universe's matter is common matter, fundamentally made out of protons and neutrons. The point by point estimations of CMB anisotropies have permitted researchers to work out the thickness of these parts with astounding accuracy.

The Vast Microwave Foundation Radiation plays had a vital impact in laying out the system for how we might interpret the universe. It has given unquestionable proof to the Theory of the universe's origin, the universe's age, and its sythesis. It has likewise directed how we might interpret the arrangement of astronomical designs, the properties of dull matter and dim energy, and the universe's initial circumstances.

In any case, the investigation of CMB stretches out past these crucial angles. The itemized estimations of CMB anisotropies keep on being a dynamic area of exploration, offering bits of knowledge into probably the most squeezing inquiries in cosmology. Here are a portion of the continuous exploration headings connected with CMB:

Early stage Gravitational Waves: Quite possibly of the most astonishing possibility in CMB research is the expected location of early stage gravitational waves. These are swells in the texture of spacetime that began in the early universe during the age of grandiose expansion. Gravitational waves are trying to distinguish, yet their engraving on the CMB can give significant experiences into the material science of the early universe and the idea of inestimable expansion. A few trials, like the BICEP/ Keck and the forthcoming Simons Observatory, expect to recognize these early stage gravitational waves.

Testing Essential Physical science: CMB information can be utilized to test basic actual speculations, like Einstein's hypothesis of general relativity. The exact estimations of CMB anisotropies can be utilized to analyze the gravitational consequences for the CMB, which might uncover deviations from the expectations of general relativity or give experiences into changed gravity hypotheses.

Planning the Huge Scope Construction: The circulation of worlds and system bunches in the universe isn't uniform however shapes a complex vast web. CMB information can be utilized to follow the appropriation of issue in the universe and study the huge scope structure. Impending analyses, similar to the Simons Observatory and the Huge Brief Review Telescope (LSST), will join CMB perceptions with enormous scope structure studies to propel how we might interpret astronomical design.

Dim Matter and Dull Energy: CMB information keeps on being an imperative instrument for grasping dim matter and dim energy, two of the most baffling parts of the universe. Progressing research plans to refine our insight into the properties of these parts and their jobs in enormous development.

Figuring out Grandiose Development: CMB information permits researchers to concentrate on the universe's set of experiences and advancement. By looking at the temperature anisotropies in the CMB, specialists can examine different vast ages, from the early universe to the current day. Progressing perceptions and examinations expect to refine how we might interpret these significant periods of grandiose development.

The field of CMB research is dynamic and steadily developing, driven by headways in innovation, information examination methods, and hypothetical models. As trials become progressively complex and informational indexes fill in size and accuracy, how we might interpret the universe will keep on extending.

Notwithstanding ground-based tests, space-based observatories have likewise made huge commitments to the investigation of CMB. The Planck satellite, sent off by the European Space Organization in 2009, was a milestone mission devoted to planning the Grandiose Microwave Foundation Radiation with remarkable accuracy. Planck's estimations have given critical bits of knowledge into the huge scope design of the universe, the conveyance of issue, and the idea of grandiose oddities.

The Planck mission noticed the CMB temperature anisotropies with outstanding precision, permitting researchers to make high-goal guides of the radiation. These guides uncovered fine subtleties in the CMB anisotropies, for example, temperature changes and polarization designs, which are important for exploring the early universe's circumstances.

One of the critical discoveries from Planck's perceptions is the affirmation of the Lambda-CDM model, which depicts the universe's arrangement as comprising of dim matter, dull energy, and standard matter. The exact estimations of the CMB by Planck have given the most dependable assurance of the universe's boundaries, including its age, creation, and the pace of its extension.

Additionally, Planck's perceptions have offered important experiences into the set of experiences and construction of the universe. The CMB information from Planck have empowered researchers to follow the universe's advancement from its initial, hot, and thick state to its present-day structure, rich with worlds, system bunches, and vast designs.

Planck's estimations have likewise upheld the hypothesis of enormous expansion, giving imperatives on inflationary models and the idea of early stage gravitational waves. The information has been instrumental in the investigation of the enormous scope circulation of issue known to mankind and the examination of vast peculiarities, like the Virus Spot, a district of the CMB with below the norm temperatures.

As innovation keeps on progressing, new analyses and observatories are not too far off, promising considerably more huge leap forwards in how we might interpret the Vast Microwave Foundation Radiation and its job in cosmology. For instance, the Simons Observatory, a ground-based explore situated in the Atacama Desert in Chile, is ready to give high-goal estimations of the CMB anisotropies and gravitational waves. It plans to resolve key inquiries in cosmology, like the idea of dull matter and dim energy.

The field of CMB research additionally converges with different areas of astronomy and cosmology, prompting interdisciplinary joint efforts and creative ways to deal with concentrating on the universe's initial history. Progressing research endeavors keep on disentangling the secrets of the universe, with the Grandiose Microwave Foundation Radiation filling in as an important and predictable wellspring of understanding.

While the Inestimable Microwave Foundation Radiation has proactively uncovered a lot of about the universe's starting points, sythesis, and development, its investigation is nowhere near total. Researchers keep on pushing the limits of our insight, utilizing perpetually modern examinations, observatories, and logical methods to refine how we might interpret the universe.

The investigation of CMB keeps on enrapturing researchers and the more extensive academic local area, as it offers a one of a kind window into the universe's outset. It associates the thick, hot early universe to the complex enormous designs we notice today. The Grandiose Microwave Foundation Radiation remains as a demonstration of human interest and the journey to unwind the most profound secrets of the universe, guaranteeing that the narrative of our universe is one that will keep on being advised for a long time into the future.

4.1 The significance of CMB in cosmology

The Infinite Microwave Foundation Radiation (CMB) is a foundation of present day cosmology, filling in as an imperative wellspring of data about the universe's initial history and its essential properties. It holds extraordinary importance in cosmology because of the abundance of information it gives about the universe, and its job in molding how we might interpret the universe couldn't possibly be more significant.

The CMB addresses the "glimmer" of the Enormous detonation, which is the predominant cosmological model for the universe's starting point. It offers a depiction of the universe's initial state, permitting researchers to explore the circumstances, structure, and development of the universe with extraordinary accuracy. This radiation, which fills the universe, is described by a few key viewpoints that make it a key part in cosmology:

Remnant of the Huge explosion: The CMB is an immediate outcome of the Theory of the universe's origin. It gives undeniable proof that the universe began from a very hot and thick state. At the point when the universe extended and cooled, it changed from a plasma of charged particles to an impartial gas, delivering the CMB as a remnant of that early state. Its presence affirms the forecasts of the Theory of prehistoric cosmic detonation and approves its focal job in grasping the universe's starting points.

Consistency and Homogeneity: The CMB displays exceptional consistency, with almost a similar temperature saw this way and that. This serious level of isotropy, where the radiation shows up similarly extraordinary from all bearings, upholds the idea that the early universe was profoundly homogeneous. The universe's homogeneity, as proven by the CMB, lines up with the expectations of the Theory of the universe's origin and fills in as an establishment for how we might interpret the universe.

Blackbody Range: The CMB's ghastly dispersion intently looks like that of a blackbody radiator. A blackbody is a romanticized object that retains and produces all frequencies of electromagnetic radiation. The CMB's blackbody range is one of the most dependable blackbody spectra at any point noticed, giving hearty proof to the Theory of the universe's origin. Its range is a finger impression of the early universe's temperature and piece.

Anisotropies: While the CMB is exceptionally uniform, it likewise shows slight temperature varieties, known as anisotropies. These anisotropies are staggeringly little, ordinarily on the request for one section in 100,000, however they convey pivotal data about the universe's initial circumstances. They act as the seeds from which vast designs, for example, systems and world bunches, framed through gravitational fascination. These anisotropies have turned into a fundamental device for concentrating for the enormous scope construction of the universe.

The CMB has significant importance in cosmology, molding how we might interpret the universe in various ways. How about we investigate a portion of the key perspectives that feature its significance:

1. **Affirmation of the Theory of prehistoric cosmic detonation:** The presence and properties of the CMB give solid affirmation of the Theory of how things came to be, which proposes that the universe started from a very hot and thick state roughly 13.8 quite a while back.

   The CMB is an immediate outcome of this early state, as it addresses the radiation that was delivered when the universe cooled and changed to an impartial gas. Its consistency and blackbody range adjust definitively with the forecasts of the Theory of the universe's origin, making it a convincing piece of proof supporting this cosmological model.

2. **Assurance of the Universe's Age:** The CMB plays had a focal impact in deciding the age of the universe. Perceptions of the CMB, alongside other cosmological estimations, have permitted researchers to compute the universe's age with exceptional accuracy. The ongoing evaluation of the universe's age, got from CMB information and different perceptions, is roughly 13.8 billion years. This assurance is a major part of how we might interpret enormous history and development.

3. **Universe's Organization:** The CMB has offered bits of knowledge into the arrangement of the universe. It has uncovered that by far most of the universe comprises of dull matter and dim energy, two perplexing parts that don't collaborate with light or different types of electromagnetic radiation. These dim constituents, alongside conventional matter (like protons and neutrons), involve the universe's matter substance. The point by point estimations of CMB anisotropies have permitted researchers to ascertain the thickness of these parts with excellent accuracy.

4. **Proof for Astronomical Expansion:** The investigation of CMB anisotropies has given significant proof on the side of the hypothesis of inestimable

expansion. Grandiose expansion places that the universe went through a fast and remarkable development in its earliest minutes, streamlining inconsistencies and giving a component to the development of enormous designs. The examples saw in CMB anisotropies, like deviations from amazing isotropy and explicit factual dispersions, adjust well to inflationary forecasts. The CMB plays had a crucial impact in propelling the inflationary model of the early universe.

5. **Enormous Scope Construction and Universe Development:** The CMB anisotropies have filled in as the seeds for the arrangement of vast designs, including cosmic systems, world groups, and superclusters. These little temperature variances, engraved in the CMB, have developed through gravitational fascination throughout enormous time, prompting the mind boggling huge scope structure we see in the universe today. The itemized investigation of CMB anisotropies has given important experiences into the arrangement and dispersion of grandiose designs.

6. **Cosmological Boundaries:** The CMB has been instrumental in refining our insight into the universe's boundaries, like the thickness of issue, the pace of the universe's development (Hubble steady), and how much dim energy. These boundaries are urgent for figuring out the universe's past and anticipating its future development. CMB estimations, related to other cosmological perceptions, have permitted researchers to decide these boundaries with expanding accuracy.

7. **Dim Matter and Dim Energy:** The CMB keeps on being an important device for researching the properties and jobs of dim matter and dim energy in the universe. Dim matter, which involves a critical part of the universe's matter substance, applies gravitational impact on the development of infinite designs. Dim energy, then again, is answerable for the universe's sped up extension. The CMB's commitment to understanding these baffling parts is integral to our perception of the universe.

8. **Requirements on Crucial Material science:** CMB information is utilized to test essential actual hypotheses, including Einstein's hypothesis of general relativity. The exact estimations of CMB anisotropies permit researchers to analyze the gravitational consequences for the CMB, which might uncover deviations from the expectations of general relativity or give experiences into adjusted gravity hypotheses. By researching the CMB, researchers have the chance to investigate the basic laws of physical science under outrageous circumstances.

9. **Planning Infinite Advancement:** The CMB information empowers researchers to follow the universe's set of experiences and development from its initial, hot, and thick state to its present-day structure, overflowing with worlds and astronomical designs. The temperature anisotropies in the CMB give a nitty gritty record of the universe's development, offering important experiences into the vast course of events and the cycles that have formed the universe.

10. **Progressing Exploration and Revelations:** The investigation of CMB keeps on being a functioning and dynamic field of examination. New investigations, observatories, and information examination methods are persistently propelling comprehension we might interpret the universe. The likely location of early stage gravitational waves, the examination of astronomical abnormalities, and the investigation of huge scope grandiose design are dynamic areas of exploration connected with the CMB.

4.2 Hypotheses linking CMB to parallel universes

Speculations connecting the Vast Microwave Foundation (CMB) to resemble universes are an intriguing and speculative part of cosmological exploration. These speculations investigate the likelihood that the CMB, which is a remainder of the early universe, could give hints or roundabout proof to the presence of equal universes or a multiverse. It's vital for note that these thoughts are still generally hypothetical and need experimental affirmation, yet they outline the innovative reasoning that drives the area of cosmology.

The idea of equal universes, frequently alluded to as the multiverse, recommends the presence of different universes or real factors past our recognizable universe. These equal universes might have different actual regulations, constants, and beginning circumstances, prompting assorted inestimable narratives and results. While the multiverse thought stays speculative, it has acquired fame in hypothetical material science because of resolving specific cosmological questions potential.

A few speculations and hypotheses have been proposed to interface the CMB to the presence of equal universes. While these thoughts are still in the domain of hypothesis, they give a provocative point of view on the connection between the CMB and the multiverse. Here, we investigate a portion of these speculations:

1. **Bubble Multiverse:**
   One theory places that our universe exists as an air pocket inside a bigger "multiverse." Each air pocket addresses an unmistakable universe with its own arrangement of actual regulations and constants. The limits between these air pocket universes might communicate with each other, possibly leaving perceptible engravings in the CMB.

   In this situation, crashes or collaborations between bubble universes could make gravitational waves or different marks that may be recognizable in the CMB. Researchers have looked for such proof in the CMB, searching for strange examples or peculiarities that could be ascribed to associations with adjoining bubble universes. While no conclusive proof has been found, the hunt proceeds, and progressions in observational innovation might give more experiences from now on.

2. **Inestimable Injury or Impact Theory:**
   Another fascinating thought proposes that our universe might have crashed into one more universe in the far off past. This impact could have made behind unmistakable imprints or "injuries" in the CMB temperature anisotropies. The examples of these temperature varieties might actually give proof of such an enormous crash.

   In this unique situation, researchers have analyzed the CMB information for strange elements that could be credited to an enormous crash. While no decisive proof has been found, this speculation features the CMB's true capacity as a device for testing the universe's set of experiences and connections with other potential domains.

3. **Equal Universes with Shifting Constants:**
   A few hypotheses inside the multiverse structure recommend that the principal constants of nature, like the speed of light or the strength of gravitational powers, may fluctuate between various equal universes. These varieties could prompt contrasts in the actual properties and conduct of every universe.

   The CMB is a vital asset for testing this speculation since it permits researchers to concentrate on the early universe's circumstances. Any varieties in the major constants would leave engraves on the CMB as particular unearthly examples or anisotropies. Analysts have directed broad looks for such varieties in the CMB information, yet up until this point, no convincing proof has arisen. The chase after factor constants in equal universes go on as an energetic area of exploration.

4. **Reflect Universes or Equality Infringement:**
   Another speculation investigates reflect universes, where particles and powers could have perfect representation partners. Such mirror universes could have various cooperations with conventional matter in our universe. This speculation is firmly connected to the idea of equality infringement, where certain actual cycles don't show reflect balance.

   The CMB is a fundamental apparatus for exploring the chance of mirror universes since it gives data about the early universe's molecule collaborations and balance breaking occasions. By concentrating on the CMB, researchers can look for inconsistencies or examples that could be credited to connections with reflect universes.

5. **Quantum Multiverse:**

Inside the structure of quantum mechanics, the idea of the multiverse emerges from the possibility that quantum occasions don't have exceptional results yet exist in superpositions of various states until noticed. Every conceivable result prompts the making of a different universe, bringing about a spreading or "many-universes" understanding of quantum mechanics.

The CMB is viewed as a possible wellspring of data about these quantum multiverses. Specialists have investigated whether the CMB anisotropies could be impacted by quantum vacillations or occasions connected with the quantum multiverse. This thought remains profoundly speculative, and no substantial proof has been tracked down in the CMB information.

While these speculations interfacing the CMB to resemble universes offer charming potential outcomes, moving toward them with a basic and wary mindset is fundamental. The multiverse idea, as a rule, stays hypothetical and testing to exactly test. Besides, any association between the CMB and equal universes is speculative and has not been authoritatively affirmed through perceptions or analyses.

In any case, these speculations represent the imaginative reasoning that drives logical investigation and the journey to figure out the idea of our universe. The CMB, as a remnant of the early universe, assumes a vital part in these speculative hypotheses since it gives a window into the universe's past and its likely collaborations with different domains.

Until this point in time, the CMB has essentially been examined to uncover experiences about the early universe, astronomical construction development, and the central properties of our universe. The amazing accuracy of CMB estimations has permitted researchers to decide the universe's age, sythesis, and the idea of dim matter and dull energy. It has additionally offered vital help for the Theory of prehistoric cosmic detonation and infinite expansion.

The CMB's utility in testing speculations connected with equal universes is as yet an open inquiry, and future progressions in observational innovation and information examination procedures might give further bits of knowledge. Meanwhile, the CMB keeps on being an essential instrument for grasping the universe's beginnings, development, and basic properties, regardless of whether its association with equal universes stays speculative.

4.3 Ongoing efforts to detect evidence

Continuous endeavors to recognize proof of grandiose microwave foundation (CMB) peculiarities and examples keep on being a huge concentration in the area of cosmology. These endeavors mean to investigate and recognize unpretentious deviations from the normal consistency and isotropy of the CMB, which could give important bits of knowledge into the early universe's set of experiences, the key laws of physical science, and, surprisingly, the presence of equal universes. While numerous parts of the CMB have been entirely considered, there are as yet unanswered inquiries and unexplained irregularities that drive progressing examination and investigation.

Vast Virus Spots:

One of the captivating peculiarities in the CMB is the presence of purported "cold spots." These are districts in the CMB sky where the temperature seems below the normal temperature of the CMB. The most renowned virus spot is the Virus Spot, an enormous and bizarrely cold locale in the southern side of the equator of the CMB. The beginning of enormous virus spots stays a subject of examination.

Progressing research endeavors center around figuring out the idea of these virus spots. Different speculations have been proposed, including the possibility that they might be brought about by connections with different universes in a multiverse situation. Albeit no conclusive proof has arisen to help these speculations, analysts keep on examining CMB information, expecting to uncover the starting points of inestimable virus spots.

CMB Anisotropies:

The CMB temperature anisotropies, which address slight temperature varieties across the inestimable microwave foundation, are specifically compelling. These anisotropies are viewed as the seeds from which inestimable designs, for example, cosmic systems and world groups, shaped through gravitational fascination.

Continuous endeavors include breaking down these anisotropies in more detail to remove extra data about the early universe. Researchers expect to distinguish any surprising examples or imbalances in the CMB anisotropies that could be characteristic of fundamental actual cycles or cooperations with other enormous areas.

Huge Scope Design Studies:

The mix of CMB information with huge scope structure studies is a strong methodology for examining the universe. Studies of universe appropriations and vast designs give corresponding data to the CMB and can assist with approving cosmological models. Progressing and forthcoming studies, for example, the Enormous Brief Overview Telescope (LSST), mean to plan the huge scope design of the universe in exceptional detail.

By contrasting the conveyance of worlds and the CMB information, researchers can acquire a more complete comprehension of vast development and the idea of dim matter and dull energy. These studies additionally give chances to look to possible connections or inconsistencies that could reveal insight into the CMB's cooperation with different universes or areas.

Look for Early stage Gravitational Waves:

The discovery of early stage gravitational waves, which are swells in the texture of spacetime produced during the enormous expansion time frame, stays a significant objective in CMB research. Gravitational waves leave an unmistakable engraving on the CMB as a particular example of polarization known as B-modes.

The BICEP/Keck cooperation and the Planck satellite have proactively directed looks for early stage gravitational waves in the CMB, yet no definitive proof has been found to date. Continuous trials, like the Simons Observatory, are explicitly intended to make exceptionally delicate estimations of the CMB's polarization to look for these subtle gravitational waves.

Planning the Reionization Age:

The CMB can likewise give bits of knowledge into the reionization age, a basic stage in the universe's set of experiences when the principal stars and worlds ionized impartial hydrogen. This cycle significantly affected the universe's straightforwardness to radiation and the development of inestimable designs.

Continuous exploration endeavors intend to refine how we might interpret the reionization age utilizing CMB information. By concentrating on the polarization of the CMB, researchers can investigate the connections between the CMB photons and the main cosmic systems and quasars. Future CMB tests, similar to the James Webb Space Telescope and the Simons Observatory, are supposed to make critical commitments to this area of examination.

Accuracy Cosmology with CMB:

The CMB keeps on being a significant asset for accuracy cosmology. Scientists use CMB information to decide crucial boundaries of the universe, like the Hubble steady, the thickness of dim matter, and the thickness of dull energy. The exactness of these estimations has worked on throughout the long term, and continuous exploration intends to additionally refine our insight into these boundaries.

This accuracy cosmology empowers researchers to test the consistency of cosmological models and recognize any deviations from the normal qualities. Any errors could give signs about new physical science or cooperations with different universes or inestimable areas.

High level Information Examination Methods:

Progressions in information examination strategies are a pivotal part of continuous CMB research. As datasets fill in size and intricacy, researchers foster complex techniques for extricating important data from CMB perceptions. Bayesian measurable strategies, AI calculations, and novel information handling methods are consistently being applied to CMB information to upgrade how we might interpret the universe.

Multi-Frequency and Multi-Courier Stargazing:

Consolidating CMB information with perceptions from different frequencies, like X-beams, radio waves, and gamma beams, considers a more extensive perspective on the universe. Multi-courier stargazing includes concentrating on the universe utilizing various sorts of signs, including electromagnetic radiation, vast beams, neutrinos, and gravitational waves.

Continuous endeavors in multi-frequency and multi-courier cosmology mean to investigate the associations between the CMB and other astrophysical peculiarities, giving a more extensive setting to grasping the universe's development and its connections with other grandiose spaces.

Global Coordinated efforts and Space Missions:

The investigation of the CMB is a worldwide undertaking, with global coordinated efforts assuming a vital part in propelling comprehension we might interpret the early universe. Space missions, for example, the European Space Office's Planck satellite and NASA's Wilkinson Microwave Anisotropy Test (WMAP), have fundamentally added to CMB research. These missions have given great CMB information and refined our insight into the universe's boundaries.

Future space missions, for example, the Astronomical Microwave Foundation Stage 4 (CMB-S4), are being developed to additionally explore the CMB's secrets. These missions will use state of the art innovation and imaginative ways to deal with CMB perception.

In outline, progressing endeavors to identify proof of enormous microwave foundation oddities and examples are a crucial part of contemporary cosmology. The CMB, as a remnant of the early universe, holds the possibility to uncover central experiences into inestimable history, the idea of dull matter and dim energy, and the presence of equal universes. While numerous parts of the CMB have been completely examined, there stay unanswered inquiries and unexplained irregularities that drive progressing examination and investigation. The union of cutting edge observational innovation, inventive information investigation strategies, and global coordinated efforts guarantees that the investigation of the CMB stays a lively and dynamic field with the commitment of additional disclosures about the idea of the universe.

Chapter 5

The Inflationary Multiverse

The Inflationary Multiverse, an entrancing and complex hypothesis in cosmology, presents a marvelous idea that extends the limits of how we might interpret the universe. This hypothesis is established in the possibility of grandiose expansion, a speculative cycle in the early universe, and the idea that our universe is only one of numerous universes inside a tremendous, interconnected multiverse.

1. **Presentation**

    The idea of a multiverse, an assortment of different universes, each with its own arrangement of actual regulations and constants, has captivated researchers and savants for a really long time. The possibility that our universe isn't exceptional and that there might exist different universes, conceivably with various properties and results, has significant ramifications for how we might interpret the universe.

    The Inflationary Multiverse, as the name recommends, is intently attached to the hypothesis of vast expansion, which was first proposed in the mid 1980s by physicist Alan Guth. Enormous expansion recommends that the universe went through a fast and dramatic extension in its initial minutes, taking care of a few well established issues in cosmology, like the skyline issue and the evenness issue. While enormous expansion has acquired significant experimental help throughout the long term, the idea of the inflationary multiverse is more speculative and stays a subject of dynamic examination and discussion inside established researchers.

2. **Astronomical Expansion**

Prior to digging into the subtleties of the inflationary multiverse, having a fundamental comprehension of the idea of infinite inflation is pivotal. Inestimable expansion is a hypothetical structure that places an early and unquestionably fast development of the universe. It was proposed as an answer for a few secrets in cosmology, and it essentially affects how we might interpret the universe's enormous scope structure.

1. **The Issues of Early Cosmology**

   Before the advancement of vast expansion, early cosmology dealt with a few critical issues. One of these was the skyline issue, which related to the perception that the infinite microwave foundation radiation, the phosphorescence of the Huge explosion, had a surprisingly uniform temperature across the whole sky. This consistency introduced a riddle since, given the limited speed of light, locales of room that gave off an impression of being causally detached shouldn't had opportunity and willpower to equilibrate their temperatures. At the end of the day, there was insufficient time for intensity to move starting with one locale then onto the next to make the inestimable microwave foundation radiation as uniform as noticed.

   The evenness issue was another issue that required tending to. This issue emerged from the perception that the universe's spatial math had all the earmarks of being exceptionally near level. Indeed, even a slight deviation from levelness would have had sensational ramifications for the universe's development, either prompting quick breakdown or perpetual extension. The inquiry was, the reason was the universe so finely tuned to be almost level?

2. **Inflationary Hypothesis**

   To resolve these issues, Alan Guth proposed the hypothesis of grandiose expansion. As per this hypothesis, in the early snapshots of the universe, a type of horrendous gravity caused a dramatic development. This development was inconceivably quick, and it happened before the universe was a subsequent old. The key thought was that this quick extension could streamline the universe and cause it to show up level, tackling the evenness issue.

   Furthermore, enormous expansion likewise tackled the skyline issue. The quick extension implied that locales of the universe that showed up causally separated were, as a matter of fact, in touch before expansion, permitting them to arrive at warm harmony and make sense of the uniform temperature of the enormous microwave foundation radiation.

   Inflationary hypothesis was additionally refined and created by different physicists, including Andrei Linde and Paul Steinhardt, and it turned into a central idea in cosmology. After some time, exact proof as perceptions of the vast microwave foundation radiation and the enormous scope construction of the universe offered solid help for the possibility of grandiose expansion.

3. **The Vital Elements of Expansion**

4.   To comprehend how expansion functions, taking into account its key ingredients is significant:

Inflaton Field: Expansion is commonly connected with the presence of a scalar field known as the inflaton field. This field has extraordinary properties that drive the fast extension of the universe. As the inflaton field develops, it can drive expansion in the early universe.

Energy Thickness: The inflaton field is described by its energy thickness. During the inflationary age, the energy thickness related with the inflaton field remains almost consistent, prompting the outstanding extension of room.

Vacuum Energy: The inflaton field is related with vacuum energy, a type of energy that emerges from the vacuum of room. This vacuum energy can drive the inflationary development.

Quantum Variances: In any event, during expansion, the laws of quantum mechanics actually apply. Quantum vacillations in the inflaton field lead to small varieties in energy thickness, which later act as the seeds for the huge scope construction of the universe.

III. The Inflationary Multiverse Speculation

Having established the groundwork with astronomical expansion, we can now direct our concentration toward the inflationary multiverse speculation. This captivating thought proposes that our universe is only one among a huge number of universes that exist inside a tremendous, interconnected multiverse. The inflationary multiverse speculation expands upon the idea of everlasting expansion, a characteristic outcome of grandiose expansion.

1. **Timeless Expansion**

   Timeless expansion, a critical component of the inflationary multiverse speculation, is an outcome of the inflaton field's properties. In districts of the universe where expansion begins, it doesn't end all the while all over the place. All things being equal, expansion resembles a chain response, and it stops in certain locales while going on in others. This outcomes in an unceasingly swelling universe where new "pocket" universes structure inside an always growing space.

2. **The Numerous Universes of the Multiverse**

   Inside the structure of timeless expansion, different pocket universes can have particular properties, like different actual constants and laws of nature. The possibility of the inflationary multiverse places that these pocket universes are basically independent universes with their own exceptional attributes. In this situation, the universe turns into a huge multiverse made out of an endless number of these pocket universes.

3. **The Multiverse Scene**

   Physicists and cosmologists frequently allude to the assortment of all conceivable pocket universes with changing properties as the "multiverse scene." The multiverse scene is immense and various, with each pocket universe addressing an alternate point inside this scene. It's urgent to comprehend that the idea of the multiverse scene is exceptionally speculative and hypothetical, yet it offers a potential answer for a few longstanding inquiries in cosmology.

IV. Proof and Difficulties

The inflationary multiverse speculation is an entrancing thought, however it stays speculative and dubious. It is essential to talk about both the proof in support of its and the difficulties it faces.

1. **Proof**

   Hypothetical Consistency: The idea of the inflationary multiverse is hypothetically reliable with the system of astronomical expansion. Everlasting expansion is a characteristic outcome of inflationary hypothesis, and the multiverse speculation is an augmentation of this thought.

   Makes sense of Calibrating: The inflationary multiverse gives a possible clarification to the tweaking of the universe's actual constants and regulations. Assuming there are a boundless number of pocket universes with various properties, it turns out to be less astounding that our universe has the particular circumstances fundamental for the presence of life.

   Testable Forecasts: A few variations of the inflationary multiverse speculation make testable expectations about the grandiose microwave foundation radiation and the huge scope design of the universe. Continuous and future perceptions might offer observational help or limitations on the multiverse thought.

2. **Challenges**

   Absence of Direct Experimental Proof: Maybe the main test confronting the inflationary multiverse speculation is the absence of direct observational proof. Distinguishing different universes inside the multiverse is a very troublesome in the event that certainly feasible errand with our ongoing innovation and comprehension of material science.

   Hypothetical Intricacy: The inflationary multiverse acquaints critical intricacy with how we might interpret the universe. It sets the presence of a huge number of universes, each with its own properties, which can be hard to accommodate with the guideline of Occam's razor.

   Testability and Falsifiability: A few pundits contend that the inflationary multiverse might be trying to test and distort, which raises worries about its status as a logical speculation. To be viewed as a logical hypothesis, a theory should be dependent upon observational testing and possibly falsifiable.

   Elective Clarifications: While the inflationary multiverse is one method for resolving inquiries of tweaking and the enormous scope design of the universe, elective clarifications exist. A few physicists and cosmologists investigate different speculations, like the human-centered rule, as an option to the multiverse theory.

V. Suggestions and Philosophical Contemplations

The inflationary multiverse, if it somehow managed to be affirmed, would have significant ramifications for how we might interpret the universe and the spot of humankind inside it. It addresses different philosophical and logical inquiries that challenge our traditional pondering the universe.

1. **Human-centered Guideline**

   The human-centered guideline, an idea firmly connected with the inflationary multiverse, proposes that the universe's actual constants and regulations are finely tuned to permit the presence of insightful life. With regards to the multiverse, the human-centered rule can be utilized to make sense of why we notice the universe's boundaries for be helpful for life. Assuming there are an endless number of pocket universes with various properties, it turns out to be less astonishing that we end up in one that upholds life.

2. **Copernican Guideline**

   The inflationary multiverse additionally challenges the Copernican rule, which recommends that we shouldn't accept any extraordinary or favored position in the universe. In a multiverse where each pocket universe might have various properties, it brings up the issue of whether our universe is extraordinary or just one among many.

3. **Cutoff points of Logical Request**

   The idea of the inflationary multiverse brings up issues about the restrictions of logical request. Might we at any point at any point expect to experimentally test or notice different universes inside the multiverse? On the off chance that not, does the multiverse thought fall outside the domain of logical examination and into the space of transcendentalism?

4. **Philosophical and Religious Contemplations**

   The idea of a multiverse has philosophical and religious ramifications. Some contend that the multiverse speculation should be visible as a naturalistic option in contrast to conventional strict cosmologies, as it gives a method for making sense of tweaking without summoning a maker. Then again, it brings up issues about the beginning of the multiverse itself and whether there might be more profound degrees of reality past it.

VI. Flow Exploration and Future Headings

The investigation of the inflationary multiverse is an area of dynamic examination inside cosmology and hypothetical physical science. Analysts keep on investigating this idea and its suggestions, while additionally looking for ways of testing its expectations.

1. **Observational Cosmology**

   One road of examination includes observational cosmology. Researchers utilize progressed telescopes and instruments to concentrate on the inestimable microwave foundation radiation and the enormous scope construction of the universe. These perceptions can give signs about the circumstances in the early universe and the presence of different universes inside the multiverse.

2. **Multiverse Models**

   Analysts are likewise creating and refining multiverse models inside the system of string hypothesis and other hypothetical structures. These models mean to give a more definite comprehension of the multiverse scene and the properties of various pocket universes.

3. **Philosophical Request**

   The idea of the multiverse keeps on moving philosophical request. Scholars, scholars, and researchers take part in conversations about the idea of the real world, the constraints of logical information, and the ramifications for how we might interpret presence.

4. **Public Commitment**

Public commitment and effort exercises assume a fundamental part in conveying the intricacies of the multiverse speculation to a more extensive crowd. Researchers and teachers work to make these ideas available and justifiable to the overall population, igniting interest and conversation.

VII. End

The Inflationary Multiverse is a convincing and questionable thought that expands the system of grandiose expansion to propose the presence of a tremendous multiverse made out of a limitless number of pocket universes. While this speculation is hypothetical and appearances challenges connected with exact testing and falsifiability, it offers expected answers for longstanding inquiries in cosmology, like the adjusting of the universe's actual constants and the huge scope design of the universe.

As exploration in cosmology and hypothetical material science progresses, we might acquire a more profound comprehension of the inflationary multiverse and its place inside our developing understanding of the universe. Whether the idea stays a speculative theory or turns into an affirmed part of our vast reality, the Inflationary Multiverse will keep on enthralling the creative mind and move philosophical and logical request long into the future.

5.1 Cosmic inflation theory and the multiverse

Vast expansion hypothesis and the multiverse are two interconnected and captivating ideas that can possibly reshape how we might interpret the universe and its beginnings. These thoughts, while not without contention and discussion, have acquired conspicuousness in the field of hypothetical material science and cosmology throughout the course of recent many years.

Astronomical expansion hypothesis, proposed by physicist Alan Guth in the mid 1980s, addresses the absolute most baffling inquiries in cosmology, especially those connected with the huge scope design and principal properties of the universe. Expansion recommends that the universe went through a dramatically quick extension in its initial minutes, tackling issues like the skyline issue and the evenness issue. It establishes the groundwork for the possibility of the multiverse, an expansion of inflationary hypothesis, which recommends that our universe is only one of innumerable universes inside a huge and interconnected multiverse.

Vast Expansion Hypothesis:

Inflationary hypothesis places that in the earliest snapshots of the universe's presence, a novel scalar field called the inflaton field drove a time of remarkable development. This development was quick to the point that it streamlined the universe's spatial math, causing it to show up level. The hypothesis of expansion additionally tended to the skyline issue, which emerges from the noticed consistency of the astronomical microwave foundation radiation across the whole sky. As indicated by the issue, locales of the universe that show up causally disengaged shouldn't had opportunity and energy to arrive at warm harmony and show such consistency.

The inflaton field's job in expansion is focal. Related with an energy thickness remains practically steady during the inflationary age, and this consistent energy thickness is liable for driving the fast extension. Quantum vacillations in the inflaton field likewise assume a pivotal part in cultivating the designs we see in the universe today.

One of the most convincing parts of expansion is that it makes explicit forecasts about the infinite microwave foundation radiation, and these expectations have been affirmed through observational proof. The examples and changes in the enormous microwave foundation radiation saw by instruments like the Planck satellite line up with the expectations of inflationary hypothesis, offering solid observational help for this system.

The Inflationary Multiverse:

The idea of the inflationary multiverse takes the possibility of inestimable expansion above and beyond by hypothesizing that our universe is only one of an endless number of universes inside a huge multiverse. This thought emerges from the idea of "timeless expansion," a characteristic result of the inflaton field's properties.

Everlasting expansion recommends that expansion doesn't end all the while wherever in the universe. All things considered, it stops in certain districts while going on in others. Thus, new "pocket" universes structure inside an always growing space. These pocket universes can have different actual constants and laws of nature, making them unmistakable from each other.

With regards to the inflationary multiverse, these pocket universes are viewed as discrete universes with their own extraordinary attributes. The multiverse speculation sets the presence of a limitless number of such universes, each dwelling in an alternate locale of the "multiverse scene," which is a portrayal of all conceivable pocket universes with fluctuating properties.

Proof and Difficulties:

The inflationary multiverse speculation is both intriguing and dubious. It offers likely answers for longstanding inquiries in cosmology, however it likewise faces critical difficulties, basically because of the absence of direct observational proof. We should investigate a portion of the proof and difficulties related with this speculation.

Proof:

Hypothetical Consistency: The idea of the inflationary multiverse is hypothetically reliable with the structure of infinite expansion. Everlasting expansion is a characteristic result of inflationary hypothesis, and the multiverse speculation is an augmentation of this thought.

Makes sense of Calibrating: The inflationary multiverse gives a likely clarification to the tweaking of the universe's actual constants and regulations. That's what it recommends assuming there are a limitless number of pocket universes with various properties, it turns out to be less astonishing that our universe has the particular circumstances important for the presence of life.

Testable Expectations: A few variations of the inflationary multiverse speculation make testable forecasts about the infinite microwave foundation radiation and the huge scope construction of the universe. Progressing and future perceptions might offer exact help or limitations on the multiverse thought.

Challenges:

Absence of Direct Exact Proof: Maybe the main test confronting the inflationary multiverse speculation is the absence of direct experimental proof. Distinguishing different universes inside the multiverse is an incredibly troublesome, on the off chance that certainly feasible, task with our ongoing innovation and comprehension of physical science.

Hypothetical Intricacy: The inflationary multiverse acquaints critical intricacy with how we might interpret the universe. It places the presence of a gigantic number of universes, each with its own properties, which can be challenging to accommodate with the standard of Occam's razor.

Testability and Falsifiability: A few pundits contend that the inflationary multiverse might be trying to test and distort, which raises worries about its status as a logical speculation. To be viewed as a logical hypothesis, a speculation should be dependent upon exact testing and possibly falsifiable.

Elective Clarifications: While the inflationary multiverse is one method for resolving inquiries of tweaking and the enormous scope construction of the universe, elective clarifications exist. A few physicists and cosmologists investigate different speculations, like the human-centered rule, as an option to the multiverse theory.

Suggestions and Philosophical Contemplations:
The idea of the inflationary multiverse has significant ramifications for how we might interpret the universe and brings up different philosophical and logical issues that challenge ordinary contemplating the universe.

Human-centered Standard: The human-centered guideline, firmly connected with the inflationary multiverse, recommends that the universe's actual constants and regulations are finely tuned to permit the presence of canny life. With regards to the multiverse, the human-centered guideline can be utilized to make sense of why we notice the universe's boundaries for be helpful for life.

Copernican Standard: The inflationary multiverse challenges the Copernican guideline, which proposes that we shouldn't expect any extraordinary or advantaged position in the universe. In a multiverse where each pocket universe might have various properties, it brings up the issue of whether our universe is special or just one among many.

Cutoff points of Logical Request: The idea of the inflationary multiverse brings up issues about the restrictions of logical request. Might we at any point at any point expect to exactly test or notice different universes inside the multiverse? On the off chance that not, does the multiverse thought fall outside the domain of logical examination and into the area of power?

Philosophical and Religious Contemplations: The idea of a multiverse has philosophical and religious ramifications. Some contend that the multiverse speculation should be visible as a naturalistic option in contrast to conventional strict cosmologies, as it gives a method for making sense of tweaking without summoning a maker. Then again, it brings up issues about the beginning of the multiverse itself and whether there might be more profound degrees of reality past it.

Ebb and flow Exploration and Future Bearings:
The investigation of the inflationary multiverse is an area of dynamic examination inside cosmology and hypothetical physical science. Specialists keep on investigating this idea and its suggestions while looking for ways of testing its expectations.

Observational Cosmology: One road of examination includes observational cosmology. Researchers utilize progressed telescopes and instruments to concentrate on the infinite microwave foundation radiation and the huge scope construction of the universe. These perceptions can give hints about the circumstances in the early universe and the presence of different universes inside the multiverse.

Multiverse Models: Scientists are likewise creating and refining multiverse models inside the structure of string hypothesis and other hypothetical systems. These models intend to give a more point by point comprehension of the multiverse scene and the properties of various pocket universes.

Philosophical Request: The idea of the multiverse keeps on moving philosophical request. Scholars, scholars, and researchers participate in conversations about the idea of the real world, the restrictions of logical information, and the ramifications for how we might interpret presence.

Public Commitment: Public commitment and effort exercises assume an essential part in imparting the intricacies of the multiverse speculation to a more extensive crowd. Researchers and instructors work to make these ideas open and justifiable to the overall population, starting interest and conversation.

5.2 Bubble universes and varying physical laws

Bubble universes and changing actual regulations are ideas that challenge the customary perspective on a solitary, uniform universe represented by predictable laws of material science. These thoughts stand out in hypothetical material science and cosmology, proposing that our universe might be only one of many, each with its own unmistakable actual properties and central constants. In this investigation, we will dig into the charming universe of air pocket universes and fluctuating actual regulations, looking at the hypothetical establishments, proof, difficulties, and ramifications of these progressive ideas.

Hypothetical Groundworks of Air pocket Universes:

The thought of air pocket universes emerges from the idea of the multiverse, which places the presence of different universes, each with its own arrangement of actual regulations and constants. In this structure, bubble universes are limited districts inside the more extensive multiverse, isolated by "bubble walls" that outline the limits of every universe. These air pocket walls can have various properties, prompting varieties in the laws of material science inside every universe.

Bubble universes can be produced through different systems, including enormous expansion and string hypothesis. One of the most notable models of air pocket universes is everlasting expansion, an augmentation of grandiose expansion, which predicts that expansion proceeds with forever in specific locales of room. In such locales, new air pocket universes are continually being framed, each with its own novel properties.

Proof and Difficulties:

Bubble universes is exceptionally theoretical and needs direct experimental proof. Notwithstanding, a few bits of roundabout proof and hypothetical contemplations loan backing to this idea:

Calibrating: One of the vital inspirations for considering bubble universes is the tweaking issue. Our universe's actual constants and regulations give off an impression of being finely tuned to take into consideration the presence of life. In the event that there are a limitless number of air pocket universes with changing properties, the human-centered rule proposes that we end up in a universe helpful for life essentially in light of the fact that life couldn't exist in universes with various boundaries.

Vast Microwave Foundation: Perceptions of the enormous microwave foundation radiation, the luminosity of the Huge explosion, have given bits of knowledge into the early universe. A few models of air pocket universes anticipate one of a kind marks in the grandiose microwave foundation that might be discernible later on, giving a likely road to experimental approval.

String Hypothesis: Air pocket universes are an idea intently attached to string hypothesis, a hypothetical system expecting to bind together the essential powers of the universe. String hypothesis proposes the presence of numerous vacuum expresses, each relating to various arrangements of actual regulations. These different vacuum states could prompt the arrangement of unmistakable air pocket universes.

Difficulties to the idea of air pocket universes include:

Absence of Exact Affirmation: The essential test is the shortfall of direct observational proof for the presence of air pocket universes. While hypothetical models might be reliable with our ongoing comprehension of material science, testing these thoughts stays a huge impediment.

Occam's Razor: The idea of air pocket universes presents an elevated degree of intricacy and, without any observational proof, brings up issues about whether it sticks to the guideline of Occam's razor, which favors less difficult clarifications over additional perplexing ones.

Multiverse or More profound Reality: Air pocket universes bring up philosophical issues about the idea of the real world. Are these air pocket universes part of a more extensive multiverse, or do they address layers of the real world, each with its own essential regulations? Understanding the real essence of these universes is a difficult errand.

Shifting Actual Regulations:

Shifting actual regulations remains closely connected with bubble universes. Assuming air pocket universes exist, they might have different basic constants and actual regulations. This idea challenges the long-held suspicion that the laws of physical science are consistent all through the universe.

In shifting actual regulations situations, the central constants that administer the way of behaving of particles and powers can fluctuate starting with one district then onto the next, prompting different actual way of behaving. For instance, the strength of gravity, the speed of light, or the majority of central particles could contrast between bubble universes or locales inside a solitary universe.

These changing actual regulations could prompt a large number of results, including the chance of various types of issue and cooperations that don't exist in our universe. This thought difficulties how we might interpret how the universe capabilities and the constraints of what is conceivable inside the domain of material science.

Proof and Difficulties:

The idea of changing actual regulations likewise needs direct observational proof. Notwithstanding, it offers a fascinating structure for resolving a few well established questions and Catch 22s in physical science:

The Idea of Constants: The upsides of key constants in our universe, like the gravitational steady or the fine-structure consistent, seem, by all accounts, to be finely tuned to consider the presence of life. Fluctuating actual regulations propose that these constants might take on various qualities in different districts or air pocket universes, possibly making sense of the noticed calibrating.

Grandiose Microwave Foundation: Like air pocket universes, models that include changing actual regulations can make forecasts about remarkable highlights in the vast microwave foundation. These forecasts might be testable through cutting edge cosmic perceptions.

Difficulties to the idea of fluctuating actual regulations include:

Intricacy and Consistency: Changing actual regulations bring intricacy into how we might interpret the universe. The test lies in fostering a system that can foresee the particular varieties in crucial constants and actual regulations across various locales or universes.

Trial Testing: Exact testing of changing actual regulations is an imposing test. To distinguish varieties in the major constants, researchers would require progressed instruments and strategies that presently don't exist.

Cutoff points of Our Universe: The idea of differing actual regulations brings up issues about the limits of our universe. Might districts with various actual regulations at any point exist together inside a similar universe, and how would they interface? Understanding the elements of such a situation is a subject of continuous exploration.

Suggestions and Philosophical Contemplations:

The ideas of air pocket universes and differing actual regulations have significant ramifications for how we might interpret the universe and bring up a scope of philosophical issues:

The Human-centered Rule: Both air pocket universes and changing actual regulations give an expected answer for the tweaking issue by conjuring the human-centered guideline. On the off chance that universes or locales exist with various properties, we wind up in one helpful for life basically in light of the fact that life couldn't exist in others.

The Idea of The real world: These ideas challenge our origination of the real world and the possibility that there is a solitary, uniform arrangement of actual regulations overseeing the whole universe. It prompts us to consider whether the truth is more intricate and multi-layered than recently envisioned.

Cutoff points of Human Information: The presence of air pocket universes and fluctuating actual regulations brings up issues about the restrictions of human information and our capacity to investigate and grasp the universe. A few parts of these ideas might remain perpetually past our compass because of mechanical and hypothetical requirements.

Philosophical and Moral Ramifications: These ideas additionally have moral and philosophical ramifications. On the off chance that the crucial laws of material science can fluctuate, it brings up issues about the idea of moral and moral standards. Do these standards additionally fluctuate across various areas of the universe?

Ebb and flow Exploration and Future Bearings:

Investigation into bubble universes and fluctuating actual regulations is a functioning and developing field inside cosmology and hypothetical material science. A few roads of examination are being sought after:

High level Perceptions: Galactic and cosmological perceptions are ceaselessly progressing. Scientists desire to find one of a kind marks in the grandiose microwave foundation or other astrophysical peculiarities that could give circuitous proof to bubble universes or differing actual regulations.

String Hypothesis: String hypothesis, which assumes a focal part in the ideas of air pocket universes and shifting actual regulations, keeps on being a focal point of exploration. String scholars try to refine and stretch out the hypothesis to all the more likely make sense of the varieties in actual regulations.

Quantum Mechanics: Investigating the association between quantum mechanics and the idea of actual regulations across various universes is an area of dynamic exploration. Understanding the quantum parts of these ideas is fundamental for their turn of events.

Philosophical Request: Thinkers and scholars participate in conversations about the philosophical ramifications of these ideas. They try to grasp the idea of the real world, the restrictions of human information, and the moral and moral ramifications of changing actual regulations.

5.3 Theoretical support and challenges

The ideas of air pocket universes and fluctuating actual regulations, while speculative and lacking direct exact proof, definitely stand out in hypothetical material science and cosmology. These thoughts challenge our conventional comprehension of the universe and its key properties. In this part, we will dive into the hypothetical help and difficulties related with these ideas.

Hypothetical Help:

Tweaking Issue: One of the focal inspirations for considering bubble universes and fluctuating actual regulations is the adjusting issue. In our universe, the upsides of principal constants and actual regulations seem, by all accounts, to be finely tuned to consider the presence of life. For instance, slight varieties in the strength of gravity or the majority of essential particles could deliver the universe aloof to life. The human-centered standard, which proposes that we wind up in a universe helpful for life since life couldn't exist in universes with various boundaries, is in many cases summoned as an answer for the tweaking issue. This point of view lines up with the idea of air pocket universes and changing actual regulations.

Enormous Microwave Foundation: Perceptions of the infinite microwave foundation radiation, the glimmer of the Huge explosion, offer a window into the early universe. A few models connected with bubble universes and differing actual regulations make explicit forecasts about extraordinary elements or examples in the grandiose microwave foundation. These forecasts might actually be tried through cutting edge galactic perceptions.

String Hypothesis: Air pocket universes and changing actual regulations are firmly connected to string hypothesis, a hypothetical structure intending to bind together the key powers of the universe. String hypothesis proposes the presence of various vacuum expresses, each comparing to various arrangements of actual regulations and principal constants. These different vacuum states could prompt the arrangement of unmistakable air pocket universes. While string hypothesis itself stays speculative and dubious, it gives a hypothetical establishment to the presence of different universes.

Challenges:

Absence of Experimental Affirmation: The main test confronting the ideas of air pocket universes and differing actual regulations is the absence of direct exact proof. While there are hypothetical inspirations and roundabout help, these thoughts stay theoretical and unsubstantiated through direct perception or trial and error. The shortfall of experimental affirmation makes it trying to lay out them as logical hypotheses.

Occam's Razor: The rule of Occam's razor, which favors less difficult clarifications over additional perplexing ones, represents a test to the idea of air pocket universes. The presentation of an endless number of universes with differing properties and actual regulations brings up issues about whether this degree of intricacy lines up with the guideline of stinginess. That's what pundits contend, without exact proof, these thoughts may be excessively mind boggling and need logical power.

Consistency and Testability: While the ideas of air pocket universes and differing actual regulations address explicit issues in physical science and cosmology, they bring intricacy into how we might interpret the universe. The test lies in fostering a system that can foresee the particular varieties in basic constants and actual regulations across various districts or universes. This consistency and testability of these thoughts are basic for their logical approval.

Moral and Philosophical Ramifications: These ideas bring up moral and philosophical issues connected with the idea of the real world and the limits of human information. For example, in the event that key constants and actual regulations can fluctuate, it prompts inquiries regarding the idea of moral and moral standards. Do these standards additionally fluctuate across various areas or universes? Tending to these philosophical ramifications can be testing and may require interdisciplinary investigation.

Multiverse or More profound Reality: The connection between bubble universes and the more extensive idea of a multiverse is a subject of continuous discussion and exploration. A few models recommend that bubble universes are essential for a bigger multiverse, while others propose they address layers of the real world, each with its own key regulations. Understanding the real essence of these universes and their relationship to the more extensive multiverse, assuming it exists, stays an area of dynamic examination.

Momentum Exploration and Future Headings:
Examination into bubble universes and differing actual regulations is ceaselessly developing and includes different roads of examination:

High level Perceptions: Galactic and cosmological perceptions keep on propelling, offering chances to find novel marks or examples in the enormous microwave foundation or other astrophysical peculiarities that might give backhanded proof to bubble universes or differing actual regulations. Forthcoming missions and telescopes are supposed to add to this undertaking.

String Hypothesis: String hypothesis, which is firmly associated with these ideas, stays a focal point of exploration inside hypothetical physical science. String scholars look to refine and stretch out the hypothesis to more readily make sense of the varieties in essential constants and actual regulations across various locales or universes.

Quantum Mechanics: Understanding the quantum parts of air pocket universes and fluctuating actual regulations is fundamental for their turn of events. Specialists are investigating the association between quantum mechanics and the idea of actual regulations across various universes, as quantum peculiarities can essentially impact these ideas.

Philosophical Request: Scholars and scholars participate in conversations about the philosophical ramifications of air pocket universes and differing actual regulations. They try to figure out the idea of the real world, the constraints of human information, and the moral and moral ramifications of shifting actual regulations. This interdisciplinary exchange adds to a more complete investigation of these thoughts.

The ideas of air pocket universes and changing actual regulations challenge our conventional comprehension of the universe and the consistency of its actual properties. While these thoughts stay speculative and unsubstantiated through direct observational proof, they offer fascinating answers for probably the most significant inquiries in cosmology and material science, especially with respect to the tweaking of the universe's actual constants.

As exploration here keeps on propelling, we might acquire a more profound comprehension of the idea of our universe and its place inside a possibly huge and different cosmological scene. Whether these ideas stay hypothetical systems or become affirmed parts of our world, the investigation of air pocket universes and differing actual regulations is a demonstration of the unfathomable interest and inventiveness of human investigation into the secrets of the universe.

Chapter 6

Quantum Computing and Parallel Processing

Quantum registering and resemble handling address two historic ideal models in the realm of figuring. While they are particular ideas, they share the shared objective of accomplishing huge jumps in computational power. In this article, we will dive into the complexities of both quantum figuring and equal handling, investigating their crucial standards, applications, and the likely ramifications for the eventual fate of innovation and science.

Quantum processing is a state of the art field of exploration that bridles the particular way of behaving of quantum mechanics to perform complex estimations at speeds that are, at times, dramatically quicker than old style PCs. It is established in the standards of superposition and entrapment, which are peculiarities remarkable to the quantum world. Superposition permits quantum bits, or qubits, to exist in different states at the same time, though snare connects the properties of at least two qubits, in any event, when they are isolated by tremendous distances. This non-instinctive nature of quantum mechanics shapes the underpinning of quantum figuring.

One of the most eminent quantum calculations is Shor's calculation, which can factor huge numbers dramatically quicker than old style calculations. Considering huge numbers is a center part of present day encryption procedures, and Shor's calculation represents an expected danger to network protection. Quantum processing can likewise fundamentally facilitate information base ventures, tackle streamlining issues, and recreate quantum frameworks, making it a flexible device with expansive applications.

Equal handling, then again, is an ordinary registering strategy that spotlights on separating a computational undertaking into more modest, reasonable sub-errands and executing them all the while utilizing various processors. This parallelism can happen at different levels, from single multi-center processors to superior execution registering bunches involving huge number of interconnected machines. Equal handling intends to boost the usage of accessible assets and work on computational productivity.

Equal processing is major in taking care of computationally concentrated issues in different spaces, like logical recreations, weather conditions determining, monetary displaying, and man-made consciousness. The capacity to separate an errand into equal strings and execute them simultaneously brings about critical decreases in execution time, rather than performing undertakings successively.

One of the vital difficulties in equal handling is accomplishing a harmony between responsibility circulation, information sharing, and synchronization. Load adjusting guarantees that all handling units work consistently, information dividing permits the trading of vital data among processors, and synchronization guarantees that strings team up productively. Accomplishing this equilibrium is basic for accomplishing the maximum capacity of equal handling.

While quantum figuring and equal handling are particular in their hidden standards and advancements, they are not totally unrelated. As a matter of fact, scientists are effectively investigating ways of consolidating the qualities of the two ideal models to make a half breed approach that use the computational force of quantum PCs close by traditional equal handling.

Quantum PCs succeed in specific kinds of issues, especially those including complex quantum frameworks and factorization. Notwithstanding, quantum equipment is still in its early stages, and building and keeping up with huge scope quantum processors presents critical specialized difficulties. Old style equal handling, then again, has proactively exhibited its proficiency in a great many applications and is a full grown innovation.

A cross breed approach that consolidates quantum and traditional figuring could outfit the qualities of the two standards while relieving their shortcomings. In this crossover model, quantum processors could be utilized for explicit quantum-related calculations, while traditional processors handle the remainder of the responsibility. By partitioning undertakings shrewdly between these two processing standards, accomplishing remarkable computational power is conceivable.

The idea of quantum parallelism is one of the essential reasons quantum figuring holds such a lot of commitment. In a traditional PC, a calculation is basically a succession of steps, executed consistently. Interestingly, quantum PCs exploit superposition to perform numerous estimations without a moment's delay.

This really intends that, hypothetically, a quantum PC could investigate all potential answers for an issue all the while, decisively lessening the time expected to track down the right response.

Consider an exemplary model known as the "mobile sales rep issue," which requests the most limited course that visits a bunch of urban communities and gets back to the beginning city. For countless urban communities, the quantity of potential courses turns out to be cosmically huge, making it infeasible for old style PCs to investigate all choices. Quantum PCs, with their inborn parallelism, can possibly find the ideal arrangement a lot quicker.

In any case, quantum parallelism accompanies a few provisos. While it considers outstanding speedup in specific calculations, the genuine speedup accomplished relies upon the particular issue and the nature of the quantum equipment. Besides, tackling quantum parallelism requires planning quantum calculations custom fitted to the novel properties of quantum bits. This requests a profound comprehension of quantum mechanics and calculation improvement, making quantum processing a many-sided field.

Equal handling in traditional figuring additionally depends on the guideline of parallelism, however it works inside the limitations of old style pieces and traditional rationale. Equal handling can include disseminating errands across numerous central processor centers, GPUs, or even across a group of PCs. In this methodology, each handling unit plays out its important for the calculation, and the outcomes are joined to deliver the ultimate result. The critical benefit of equal handling is that it can altogether diminish execution time for errands that can be separated into more modest, autonomous sub-assignments.

The commonsense execution of equal handling requires cautious thought of a few elements, including responsibility dissemination, information correspondence, and synchronization. Load adjusting guarantees that each handling unit has a generally equivalent measure of work to do, keeping a few units from standing by while others are over-burden. Information dividing components empower proficient correspondence among handling units, guaranteeing they approach the vital data. Synchronization is critical to facilitate the execution of strings or cycles to stay away from clashes and guarantee proficient cooperation.

The decision between quantum figuring and old style equal handling relies upon the idea of the issue to be settled. A few issues are intrinsically appropriate for quantum registering, while others can be effectively dealt with through old style equal handling. For instance, quantum PCs are supposed to succeed in errands like mimicking quantum frameworks, streamlining complex frameworks, and considering enormous numbers. Interestingly, old style equal handling is more qualified for undertakings that include a serious level of information handling, for example, picture and video delivering, information investigation, and AI.

Lately, scientists have started investigating the idea of a quantum-traditional crossover approach. In this methodology, quantum processors handle explicit quantum-related calculations, while old style processors deal with the leftover responsibility. The thought is to take advantage of the qualities of quantum registering where it succeeds while utilizing old style equal handling until the end of the undertakings.

The crossover model can possibly give a sober minded answer for a portion of the ongoing constraints of quantum figuring. Quantum equipment is still in its formative stages, and keeping up with stable quantum states in enormous scope quantum processors stays a test. Quantum blunder rectification is a basic area of exploration to make quantum processors more dependable, however it accompanies extra above as far as qubits and tasks. Old style processors, then again, are vigorous and deeply grounded.

Carrying out a half and half model requires proficient connection points between the quantum and old style parts. Quantum-old style cross breed calculations and programming systems should be created to split undertakings successfully and guarantee consistent joint effort among quantum and traditional processors. As quantum equipment develops and turns out to be all the more promptly accessible, cross breed processing might turn into the extension among old style and quantum figuring, empowering useful and versatile answers for many issues.

The possible utilizations of quantum registering and equal handling length across different fields, from cryptography and money to logical examination and man-made reasoning. We should investigate a portion of the key regions where these ideal models are having a massive effect.

Cryptography:

Quantum figuring presents both a danger and an answer for cryptography. Shor's calculation, a quantum calculation, can productively factor enormous numbers, which could think twice about utilized encryption strategies like RSA. Then again, quantum-safe encryption procedures are being created to endure quantum assaults. Quantum key dispersion (QKD) is a quantum cryptography method that utilizes the standards of quantum mechanics to get correspondence channels.

Logical Recreation:

Quantum PCs can possibly alter logical reproductions, especially in the field of quantum science and materials science. Reproducing the way of behaving of perplexing quantum frameworks, like sub-atomic associations and material properties, can give significant bits of knowledge to tranquilize disclosure, materials plan, and principal logical examination.

Streamlining Issues:

Some certifiable issues include tracking down the best arrangement from countless potential outcomes, for example, improving inventory network planned operations, portfolio the board, and energy lattice the executives.

Quantum figuring is appropriate for tackling advancement issues all the more productively, which can prompt expense investment funds and further developed navigation.

AI and Computerized reasoning:

AI calculations frequently include preparing complex models on enormous datasets, which can be computationally serious. Equal handling speeds up the preparation cycle by disseminating undertakings across various handling units, diminishing preparation times. Quantum registering, with its true capacity for quicker calculation execution, holds guarantee for further developing AI calculations and empowering the advancement of new computer based intelligence models.

Weather conditions Guaging:

Weather conditions guaging models require huge computational ability to process immense measures of climatic information. Equal handling assumes a pivotal part in running these recreations productively, permitting meteorologists to give more exact and convenient figures.

Monetary Demonstrating:

Monetary establishments utilize equal handling to run risk evaluations, perform portfolio advancements, and execute high-recurrence exchanging calculations. Proficient equal handling empowers quicker navigation and can altogether affect monetary business sectors.

Drug Revelation:

Quantum registering can help with recreating complex sub-atomic collaborations and speeding up the medication disclosure process. By displaying the way of behaving of particles and their collaborations with expected drugs, specialists can recognize new possibility for drug improvement all the more proficiently.

Energy Matrix The board:

Overseeing current energy matrices productively requires tackling complex advancement issues connected with energy age, circulation, and request. Quantum registering and resemble handling can assist with tracking down ideal answers for energy matrix the board, lessening costs and further developing maintainability.

Information Investigation and Huge Information Handling:

Dealing with and breaking down huge datasets are normal difficulties in different fields, including business examination, genomics, and web-based entertainment. Equal handling methods are pivotal for circulating information handling errands and accomplishing convenient bits of knowledge from tremendous information sources.

Computerized reasoning and Advanced mechanics:

Equal handling is essential in the improvement of man-made intelligence frameworks and mechanical technology. It empowers constant information handling, direction, and control in independent vehicles, modern robots, and brilliant gadgets.

Both quantum figuring and resemble handling can possibly change businesses and logical exploration. Notwithstanding, a few difficulties and limits should be addressed to understand their potential completely.

On account of quantum figuring, one of the essential difficulties is qubit strength. Quantum pieces are exceptionally delicate to ecological factors, and keeping up with their quantum states for broadened periods is a mind boggling task. Quantum mistake adjustment is a functioning area of exploration, however it requires extra qubits to encode and address quantum data, making quantum processors bigger and more testing to assemble.

Besides, increasing quantum equipment to deal with down to earth, huge scope issues stays a considerable errand. The improvement of shortcoming open minded quantum processors is fundamental for the inescapable reception of quantum registering. Analysts are investigating different actual stages for qubits, for example, superconducting circuits, caught particles, and topological qubits, each with its own arrangement of benefits and difficulties.

With regards to resemble handling, accomplishing ideal burden adjusting and proficient information sharing can be perplexing, particularly for sporadic or dynamic jobs. Also, synchronizing strings or cycles across different processors can present above and bottlenecks. These difficulties require cautious plan and enhancement of equal calculations and models.

Both quantum figuring and equal handling likewise face the test of energy productivity. As computational requests keep on developing, power utilization turns into a basic concern. Quantum PCs, specifically, require very low temperatures to work, which represents extra energy and foundation necessities.

One more significant thought is the improvement of programming and calculations that can successfully use quantum registering and equal handling assets. Developers and analysts need to adjust to new programming models, apparatuses, and dialects to make the most of these standards.

Taking everything into account, quantum registering and equal handling are two strong processing ideal models with the possibility to reshape the mechanical scene. Quantum figuring tackles the standards of quantum mechanics to perform estimations at speeds recently considered inconceivable, while equal handling separates assignments into more modest units, enhancing computational proficiency. Their applications length across a great many fields, from cryptography and logical examination to man-made brainpower and monetary demonstrating.

The eventual fate of figuring might well lie in a mixture model that consolidates the qualities of both quantum and old style handling. Quantum-old style half and half figuring offers a commonsense answer for the ongoing impediments of quantum equipment, considering versatile and effective answers for complex issues.

Notwithstanding the promising progressions in quantum registering and equal handling, huge difficulties still need to be tended to, including qubit steadiness, adaptability, energy proficiency, and the improvement of fitting programming and calculations. As innovation keeps on propelling, it is critical for specialists, designers, and pioneers to cooperate to open the maximum capacity of these processing ideal models and shape a future where beforehand recalcitrant issues can be handled with extraordinary proficiency. The cooperative energy among quantum and traditional handling might well lead us into another time of computational abilities, altering businesses and our comprehension of the world.

6.1 Introduction to quantum computing

Quantum figuring is a progressive field in the domain of calculation, offering the possibility to take care of complicated issues at speeds that old style PCs can merely fantasize about. This presentation will investigate the essential standards and ideas of quantum registering, giving an outline of its authentic setting, the hidden quantum mechanics, and the possible applications and suggestions for the eventual fate of innovation and science.

At its center, quantum registering use the special and frequently unreasonable properties of quantum mechanics to perform calculations. Dissimilar to traditional PCs, which use pieces to address data as one or the other 0 or 1, quantum PCs use quantum bits, or qubits, which can exist in numerous states all the while because of a peculiarity called superposition. Superposition permits qubits to be in a mix of 0 and 1 states, extraordinarily expanding the computational force of quantum frameworks.

This one of a kind property of qubits is supplemented by another fundamental quantum idea, entrapment. Trap connects the properties of at least two qubits, in any event, when they are isolated by tremendous distances. This implies that the condition of one qubit can momentarily impact the condition of another, making the potential for profoundly productive and interconnected quantum frameworks.

Quantum processing follows its foundations back to the mid twentieth century when quantum mechanics was first planned. Spearheading physicists like Max Planck, Albert Einstein, Niels Bohr, and Erwin Schrödinger fostered the underpinnings of quantum mechanics, which portrayed the way of behaving of particles at the nuclear and subatomic scale. As the comprehension of quantum mechanics advanced, obviously these standards could reform figuring.

In the mid 1980s, physicist Richard Feynman proposed the possibility of quantum PCs as a way to effectively reproduce quantum frameworks. He noticed that traditional PCs attempted to mimic quantum peculiarities precisely because of the dramatic intricacy of the estimations in question. This knowledge established the hypothetical starting point for quantum processing, recommending that quantum frameworks could normally take care of issues that were computationally recalcitrant for traditional machines.

Nonetheless, it was only after the 1990s that the field of quantum figuring really started to come to fruition. Canadian physicist David Deutsch presented the idea of a widespread quantum PC, a machine fit for mimicking any actual framework, including other quantum PCs. This thought extended the conceivable outcomes of quantum processing, underscoring its true capacity as a flexible device for tackling many issues.

In 1994, Peter Shor, a mathematician at AT&T Ringer Research facilities, presented Shor's calculation. This weighty calculation showed the way that a quantum PC could factor huge numbers dramatically quicker than the most popular old style calculations. Considering huge numbers is a major test in cryptography, and Shor's calculation represented a critical danger to traditional encryption strategies. All the while, Lov Grover, an IBM scientist, fostered Grover's calculation, which could look through unsorted information bases a lot quicker than old style PCs. These leap forwards ignited serious interest in the viable applications and possible effect of quantum registering.

Quantum processing innovations have since cutting edge impressively. Analysts and organizations overall are effectively attempting to foster quantum equipment, programming, and calculations. Remarkable quantum registering stages, for example, IBM's Quantum Experience, Google's Quantum simulated intelligence lab, and new businesses like Rigetti and D-Wave, have arisen, offering admittance to quantum PCs through cloud administrations. These stages have sped up exploration and trial and error in quantum figuring, making it more open to a more extensive local area of researchers and specialists.

Quantum figuring holds enormous commitment in different fields. Quite possibly of its most convincing application lies in cryptography. Shor's calculation's capacity to factor enormous numbers dramatically quicker than traditional calculations represents a critical test to the security of broadly utilized encryption techniques. Subsequently, quantum-safe encryption methods are being created to defend information and correspondences in the post-quantum period. Quantum key dissemination (QKD) is a quantum cryptography procedure that utilizes the standards of quantum mechanics to get correspondence channels, making it for all intents and purposes safe to quantum assaults.

Another key region where quantum registering can have a significant effect is logical reenactments. Quantum PCs are especially appropriate for reproducing quantum frameworks and materials, which are fundamental in fields like science and materials science. For instance, quantum PCs can effectively display atomic communications, substance responses, and the way of behaving of complicated materials, prompting progressions in drug revelation, materials plan, and the comprehension of key actual cycles.

Advancement issues, pervasive in different businesses, can likewise profit from quantum processing. Issues that include tracking down the best arrangement from countless potential outcomes, for example, improving stockpile chains, monetary portfolios, and energy framework the board, can be handled all the more proficiently with quantum calculations.

Quantum PCs succeed at investigating numerous arrangement competitors all the while, which can prompt expense reserve funds, further developed navigation, and asset portion.

AI and computerized reasoning (artificial intelligence) are encountering critical development, and quantum processing is ready to assume a crucial part in propelling these fields. AI calculations frequently include preparing complex models on huge datasets, which can be computationally serious. Quantum registering can speed up AI errands by giving quicker calculation execution, empowering the advancement of all the more impressive artificial intelligence models and speeding up the speed of exploration in man-made intelligence and mechanical technology.

Weather conditions estimating is another space where quantum registering can upset expectations. Weather conditions models depend on handling huge measures of climatic information and running complex reproductions. Quantum registering, with its capacity to deal with enormous datasets and perform rapid estimations, can possibly improve the precision and idealness of weather conditions figures, a fundamental part of calamity readiness and asset the board.

In the monetary area, quantum processing can improve risk appraisal, portfolio the board, and high-recurrence exchanging calculations. The productive investigation of monetary information can fundamentally affect market strength and venture choices. Besides, the advancement of quantum calculations for monetary displaying might open up new open doors for additional precise expectations and further developed techniques in the monetary business.

Energy network the board presents a progression of intricate improvement issues connected with energy age, circulation, and request. Quantum figuring, alongside its true capacity for quicker and more proficient calculations, can assist with tracking down ideal answers for energy matrix the board, at last prompting cost reserve funds and a more maintainable energy framework.

Information examination and huge information handling are significant in different spaces, including business investigation, genomics, and online entertainment. Overseeing and examining huge datasets proficiently is fundamental for removing important experiences. Quantum figuring's velocity and equal handling abilities can offer huge benefits in handling, examining, and getting experiences from monstrous information sources.

Man-made reasoning and advanced mechanics stand to profit from quantum processing too. Quantum PCs can handle information and settle on choices progressively, a basic necessity for independent vehicles, modern robots, and savvy gadgets. This can prompt more secure and more productive independent frameworks that can work in mind boggling and dynamic conditions.

While quantum figuring can possibly achieve groundbreaking changes in these and different areas, it isn't without its difficulties. One of the main difficulties is qubit steadiness. Quantum pieces are exceptionally delicate to natural elements, which can cause qubits to lose their quantum states. Keeping up with stable quantum states overstretched periods is an intricate errand, and specialists are effectively investigating techniques to improve qubit security.

Quantum mistake revision is one more basic area of examination. It is fundamental for make quantum processors more dependable. Mistake rectification includes encoding quantum data in a manner that permits blunders to be distinguished and revised. Be that as it may, executing blunder rectification requires extra qubits and computational above, making it a non-inconsequential test.

The versatility of quantum equipment is a principal issue. Fabricating and keeping up with huge scope quantum processors is in fact testing. Increasing quantum PCs to deal with commonsense, enormous scope issues requires tending to actual impediments, qubit availability, and limiting the impacts of commotion and obstruction.

One more test lies in the energy effectiveness of quantum processing. Quantum PCs require very low temperatures to work, which includes significant energy utilization. Dealing with the energy prerequisites of quantum frameworks is a continuous worry, as it impacts both the ecological effect and the reasonableness of quantum equipment.

Creating quantum programming and calculations that can really use quantum registering assets is significant. Software engineers and scientists should adjust to new programming models, instruments, and dialects intended for quantum registering. Besides, quantum-traditional mixture registering approaches are arising as a functional answer for capitalize on both quantum and old style assets, improving the common sense of quantum figuring.

6.2 The potential impact on computational capabilities

The expected effect of progressing computational abilities, driven by arising advances and developments, is huge and groundbreaking. As we push the limits of what is conceivable in the domain of calculation, our capacity to tackle complex issues, further develop navigation, and drive advancement across different areas is growing at an extraordinary rate. In this investigation, we will dig into the expected effect of improved computational abilities in key regions, from logical exploration and medical care to business and training, at last reshaping the manner in which we live and work in the computerized age.

1. **Logical Exploration and Disclosure:**

   Upgraded computational abilities are changing logical exploration and disclosure. In fields, for example, astronomy, environment displaying, and atomic science, scientists are tackling the force of superior execution figuring to mimic and examine complex peculiarities.

   With quicker and more modern calculations, researchers can demonstrate the way of behaving of systems, anticipate environment designs, and reproduce the communications of proteins, propelling comprehension we might interpret the universe and life itself.

   For instance, in the domain of genomics, computational progressions have prepared for customized medication and accuracy medical care. DNA sequencing and examination, once staggeringly tedious and costly, have become quicker and more practical, empowering the distinguishing proof of hereditary inclinations to sicknesses and the advancement of custom fitted therapy plans.

   In materials science, high level recreations and computational models permit specialists to plan new materials with exceptional properties for different applications, from lightweight and strong materials for aviation to energy-productive materials for hardware. The capacity to speed up logical examination and disclosure through computational displaying and reenactments can possibly prompt historic developments and mechanical headways.

2. **Medical services and Life Sciences:**

Computational capacities significantly affect medical services and life sciences. Clinical imaging, drug disclosure, and patient consideration have all profited from computational advances. Clinical imaging advances, for example, X-ray and CT filters, produce high-goal pictures that guide in the early discovery and finding of sicknesses. AI calculations applied to clinical imaging can recognize peculiarities and help radiologists in giving exact evaluations.

Drug disclosure is another region where computational capacities are driving advancement. Specialists can utilize recreations and calculations to show the collaborations between potential medication compounds and organic targets. This speeds up the medication disclosure process, lessens expenses, and improves the probability of distinguishing powerful therapies for different sicknesses, including malignant growth and irresistible infections.

In understanding consideration, electronic wellbeing records (EHRs) and clinical choice emotionally supportive networks (CDSS) influence computational ability to further develop medical care conveyance and patient results. EHRs smooth out understanding information the executives, while CDSS gives medical care experts proof based proposals, at last prompting more educated clinical choices.

The combination of computational abilities with medical care is additionally powering the improvement of telemedicine, wearable wellbeing gadgets, and remote checking frameworks, furnishing patients with more noteworthy admittance to medical care benefits and working with early intercession and counteraction.

3. **Business and Industry:**

Upgraded computational abilities are changing the manner in which organizations and businesses work. From information examination to store network improvement, organizations are utilizing information pushed bits of knowledge to acquire a serious brink. Huge information investigation, controlled by elite execution processing, permits associations to remove significant data from immense datasets, empowering better navigation, customized advertising, and further developed client encounters.

Man-made brainpower (artificial intelligence) and AI are reshaping businesses via mechanizing processes, further developing productivity, and empowering prescient examination. In assembling, simulated intelligence driven mechanical technology and computerization are upgrading efficiency and accuracy. In finance, simulated intelligence fueled calculations are making high-recurrence exchanging more modern and proficient.

Store network enhancement is another region where computational capacities are having a tremendous effect. By using information and high level calculations, organizations can upgrade their stock chains, diminishing expenses, limiting waste, and guaranteeing convenient conveyances.

The combination of computational capacities with the business scene is encouraging advancement and the improvement of new items and administrations. It is likewise prompting the rise of new plans of action and ventures, like the sharing economy and the Web of Things (IoT).

4. **Schooling and Learning:**

In the field of training, improved computational capacities are opening up new open doors for learning and educating. The incorporation of innovation into homerooms and online schooling stages is extending admittance to instructive assets and cultivating customized growth opportunities. Instructive foundations are utilizing computational devices to establish vivid virtual learning conditions, making schooling really captivating and intuitive.

Information investigation and AI are being applied to instructive information to evaluate understudy execution, recognize regions where understudies might require extra help, and give customized suggestions to progress. This approach can assist instructors with fitting their instructing strategies to individual understudy needs.

Also, computational reproductions are upgrading the investigation of complicated subjects, like physical science, science, and science, by empowering understudies to lead tries and investigate logical peculiarities in virtual conditions. These computerized instruments add to a more profound comprehension of ideas and support involved learning.

The likely effect of computational capacities on instruction stretches out past conventional homerooms. Online courses and remote learning are turning out to be more available, furnishing individuals with amazing open doors for deep rooted mastering and expertise advancement. By and large, computational advancements are reshaping the schooling scene and making learning more comprehensive and versatile.

5. **Ecological Maintainability:**

Tending to worldwide ecological difficulties, for example, environmental change and asset preservation, depends on improved computational abilities. Environment displaying and recreation, fueled by supercomputers, assume a crucial part in understanding environment designs, foreseeing cataclysmic events, and evaluating the effect of human exercises on the climate.

Computational apparatuses are likewise essential in the advancement of practical energy arrangements. High level reenactments empower analysts to plan more productive sunlight powered chargers, wind turbines, and energy stockpiling frameworks. These innovations are adding to the change to cleaner and more reasonable wellsprings of energy.

Furthermore, computational capacities are being utilized in accuracy horticulture, where information examination and sensor advances assist ranchers with upgrading crop the board, lessen asset squander, and further develop yields. By boosting asset proficiency, computational farming practices add to food security and ecological supportability.

6. **Space Investigation and Cosmology:**

Computational capacities have fundamentally progressed space investigation and cosmology. In space investigation, superior execution processing is imperative for mission arranging, direction estimations, and reenactments of space apparatus conduct. Complex estimations are expected to explore shuttle to far off planets, moons, and space rocks, as well as to break down information from space missions.

Stargazing benefits from computational advances by handling and investigating huge datasets got from telescopes and space-based observatories. Analysts can reproduce divine peculiarities, model the development of cosmic systems, and quest for exoplanets and indications of extraterrestrial life. Computational stargazing is at the front of our mission to figure out the universe and uncover its secrets.

7. **Public safety and Protection:**

The likely effect of improved computational capacities on public safety and safeguard is significant. Guard organizations depend on supercomputers and high level recreations for key preparation, insight examination, and the improvement of military innovations. Superior execution registering helps with the displaying of military situations, improving planned operations, and mimicking the presentation of protection frameworks.

Network safety is another basic region where computational capacities are of foremost significance. The improvement of cutting edge encryption and unscrambling methods, as well as the location and anticipation of digital dangers, depends on strong registering assets. Computational calculations are fundamental in recognizing weaknesses, safeguarding basic foundation, and shielding delicate data.

The utilization of man-made reasoning and AI for danger location and independent frameworks is changing the guard business. Independent vehicles, automated ethereal frameworks, and front line advanced mechanics are instances of military innovations that advantage from computational capacities.

8. **Diversion and Media:**

The diversion and media industry is going through a computerized transformation fueled by computational capacities. Film and video creation depend on refined PC produced symbolism (CGI) and embellishments. Computerized activity, 3D displaying, and augmented reality encounters have become vital to media outlets, offering crowds vivid and enamoring narrating.

6.3 Security challenges in a world of quantum computing

The rise of quantum registering has introduced another time of computational power, promising to change fields like cryptography, materials science, and streamlining. In any case, with the expected advantages of quantum processing come critical security challenges. This exposition investigates the security challenges that emerge in a universe of quantum processing, zeroing in on the ramifications for cryptography, information security, and the requirement for post-quantum cryptography arrangements.

1. **Cryptographic Weaknesses:**
   One of the most squeezing security challenges presented by quantum registering is its capability to break generally utilized cryptographic frameworks. Numerous encryption techniques, like RSA and ECC (Elliptic Bend Cryptography), depend on the trouble of calculating enormous numbers or tackling discrete logarithm issues. Quantum PCs, strikingly Shor's calculation, can tackle these issues dramatically quicker than old style PCs. Subsequently, the security of computerized correspondence and information assurance could be compromised.

   This danger to cryptography has sweeping ramifications. Privacy, honesty, and validation in different web-based exchanges, including secure correspondence, online business, and monetary administrations, could be risked. Associations, states, and people should plan for a post-quantum world by creating and conveying quantum-safe encryption techniques.

2. **Post-Quantum Cryptography:**
   The turn of events and execution of post-quantum cryptography is a significant reaction to the cryptographic weaknesses presented by quantum registering. Present quantum cryptography alludes on cryptographic calculations and conventions that are intended to endure assaults by quantum PCs. Scientists and cryptographers are effectively dealing with the improvement of such calculations.

   Post-quantum cryptography incorporates different methodologies, including grid based cryptography, code-based cryptography, and hash-based cryptography. These methodologies mean to give protection from quantum assaults while staying viable and productive for certifiable applications. Guaranteeing a smooth progress from existing cryptographic frameworks to post-quantum arrangements is an intricate test that should be painstakingly made due.

   State run administrations and associations are urged to screen the advancement of post-quantum cryptography research and get ready for the inevitable change to safer encryption norms.

3. **Quantum-Safe Cryptographic Conventions:**
   Past creating post-quantum cryptographic calculations, getting advanced correspondence additionally requires the improvement of quantum-safe crypto-

graphic conventions. These conventions are intended to safeguard information during transmission and capacity in this present reality where enemies might approach quantum registering assets.

Quantum-safe cryptographic conventions frequently depend on deep rooted procedures like symmetric key encryption, advanced marks, and secure key trade. These methodologies offer protection from quantum assaults and can be coordinated into existing correspondence frameworks.

The execution of quantum-safe cryptographic conventions is fundamental for protecting delicate data in the present and during the progress to post-quantum cryptographic guidelines.

4. **Key Administration:**

One more basic part of safety in a quantum registering climate is key administration. Conventional key trade strategies, for example, those utilized in the Diffie-Hellman key trade, may become powerless against quantum assaults. The test lies in safeguarding encryption keys from being undermined by quantum foes.

Quantum key dissemination (QKD) is a quantum cryptographic strategy that use the standards of quantum mechanics to get key trade. QKD depends on the identification of quantum properties, like snare, to make secure encryption keys. It gives an elevated degree of safety, even within the sight of quantum PCs, and offers a promising answer for key administration in a quantum registering world.

Associations need to consider carrying out key administration arrangements that are quantum-safe and equipped for safeguarding delicate information in a post-quantum climate.

5. **Quantum-Safe Equipment:**

Quantum figuring not just represents a danger to existing cryptographic strategies yet in addition raises worries about the security of equipment based security frameworks. Quantum foes might actually take advantage of weaknesses in cryptographic equipment to think twice about.

Quantum-safe equipment intends to address these weaknesses by giving alter safe and quantum-safe security arrangements. This incorporates secure equipment modules that can safeguard cryptographic keys and information. Secure equipment plan and assembling processes are fundamental to guarantee the uprightness of quantum-safe equipment.

Associations that depend on equipment based security systems ought to consider executing quantum-safe answers for safeguard their basic resources.

6. **Quantum-Safe Conventions for Blockchain and Digital currencies:**

Cryptographic forms of money and blockchain innovation have acquired boundless prevalence as of late. Be that as it may, the security of blockchain networks and computerized monetary forms is in danger in a quantum figuring time. Blockchain exchanges and wallets could be powerless against assaults by quantum PCs, possibly compromising the respectability and security of digital currency exchanges.

To address these worries, quantum-safe conventions for blockchain and digital currencies are being created. These conventions expect to improve the security of blockchain networks by giving encryption techniques and advanced marks that are hearty against quantum assaults.

Cryptographic money clients, financial backers, and blockchain engineers ought to remain educated about the advancement regarding quantum-safe conventions and consider embracing them to safeguard their computerized resources.

7. **Expanded Online protection Dangers:**

The approach of quantum processing presents new elements of network safety gambles. Quantum foes, with admittance to strong quantum PCs, can send off assaults that were already infeasible. As well as breaking encryption and cryptographic conventions, quantum PCs might possibly take advantage of weaknesses in programming and equipment security systems.

Associations should adjust to this developing danger scene by putting resources into cutting edge online protection measures. This incorporates routinely refreshing and fixing programming, carrying major areas of strength for out controls, and directing security reviews to recognize and relieve weaknesses that could be taken advantage of by quantum foes.

8. **Quantum-Safe Cryptanalysis:**

As quantum processing develops, it isn't just a danger to traditional cryptographic frameworks yet additionally an instrument for likely enemies to foster new cryptanalytic methods. Quantum foes might have the option to take advantage of shortcomings in cryptographic calculations that were not initially intended to endure quantum assaults.

Cryptanalysts and security specialists are effectively exploring quantum-safe encryption techniques, however associations should stay careful and proactive in safeguarding their information and correspondence. Consistently refreshing encryption guidelines and conventions can assist with moderating the gamble of cryptanalysis.

9. **Moral and Administrative Contemplations:**

The security difficulties of quantum processing stretch out past innovation to moral and administrative contemplations. The likely ramifications of quantum processing on protection, reconnaissance, and advanced freedoms should be painstakingly analyzed and tended to.

Moral contemplations include issues, for example, the dependable utilization of quantum processing capacities, the security of individual protection, and the possible effect on common freedoms. It is essential for policymakers, lawful specialists, and innovation partners to participate in conversations on the best way to guarantee moral and capable utilization of quantum registering advances.

According to an administrative viewpoint, states might have to lay out legitimate systems and norms for quantum-safe cryptography and safety efforts. Empowering industry joint effort and global collaboration on quantum security guidelines will be fundamental.

10. **Quantum Registering as a Protection System:**

While quantum figuring presents security challenges, it likewise offers the potential for new security systems. Quantum cryptography, like QKD, can give solid encryption keys and secure correspondence channels. These quantum-based security arrangements can be utilized to safeguard basic framework, government interchanges, and delicate information.

Associations and states ought to investigate the utilization of quantum innovations as a safeguard component against potential dangers presented by quantum enemies.

Chapter 7

Altered States of Consciousness

Modified conditions of cognizance, a domain of human experience that has entranced and confused people since the beginning of time, have been the subject of philosophical, logical, and mysterious request. These modified states include many peculiarities, from the ordinary encounters of dreaming and staring off into space to the exceptional domains got to through contemplation, drug-incited states, and other changed states. Understanding modified conditions of cognizance is a complicated and complex undertaking that requires an investigation of the mental, neurological, and social aspects that shape how we might interpret these states. This article tries to investigate the idea of modified conditions of awareness, its set of experiences, different structures, fundamental systems, and social importance.

Changed conditions of cognizance are in a general sense unique in relation to common waking cognizance, a perspective that most people insight consistently. In the normal waking state, we are ready, objective, and mindful of our environmental elements. Our impression of the outer world and our inward considerations and feelings are moderately steady and persistent. In any case, adjusted states upset this soundness, prompting changes in discernment, cognizance, and profound experience. These states can be instigated through different means, including reflection, spellbinding, tactile hardship, rest, and the utilization of psychoactive substances.

One of the most widely recognized and all around concentrated on modified conditions of awareness is dreaming. At the point when we dream, we enter an interesting condition of cognizance portrayed by distinctive tactile encounters, frequently inconsequential to the outside world, and an absence of cognizant command over the fantasy story. Dreams can be lovely, terrifying, odd, or everyday, and they frequently highlight a cast of characters and settings that contrast from our cognizant existence. Analysts have investigated the substance and importance of dreams for a really long time, and different speculations have been proposed to make sense of their capability and importance.

Sigmund Freud, one of the trailblazers of present day brain research, accepted that fantasies were the "illustrious street to the oblivious." He contended that fantasies were the brain's approach to handling subdued wants and nerves, giving a window into the secret operations of the mind. Freud's translation of dreams accentuated sexual and forceful topics, recommending that our most taboo cravings tracked down articulation in the representative language of dreams. While a large number of Freud's particular thoughts have become undesirable in contemporary brain research, his accentuation on the significance of the oblivious psyche and the emblematic idea of dream content keeps on impacting the investigation of dreams.

Different clinicians have proposed elective speculations to make sense of the capability of dreams. Some propose that fantasies act as a type of critical thinking, permitting the psyche to deal with through irritating problems and track down clever fixes to issues. Others contend that fantasies have a more versatile capability, assisting us with handling feelings and solidify recollections. In spite of the different hypotheses about the motivation behind dreams, their review stays a rich area of exploration in brain research and neuroscience.

Wandering off in fantasy land is one more typical type of adjusted awareness that a great many people experience consistently. Not at all like the vivid and frequently unusual nature of dreams, fantasizes commonly include unconstrained, mind-meandering considerations that can happen during calm minutes in regular day to day existence. Fantasies can be a wellspring of motivation, an approach to intellectually practice future occasions, or a method for briefly getting away from the requests of the current second. They frequently include elaborate dreams, where people envision themselves in various situations and circumstances, here and there investigating their most profound cravings or fears.

While fantasizing may appear as though a trifling or irrelevant part of human cognizance, it has gotten consideration from specialists keen on its mental and close to home importance. Studies have shown that staring off into space is related with innovativeness, critical thinking, and, surprisingly, further developed mind-set. In any case, extreme wandering off in fantasy land, frequently alluded to as maladaptive fantasizing, can slow down day to day working and might be a side effect of basic mental issues.

Reflection addresses an intentional and precise work to modify one's condition of cognizance. It includes the act of concentrating, frequently on a particular item, thought, or sensation, fully intent on accomplishing an elevated condition of mindfulness and inward peacefulness. Contemplation has a long history, with establishes in strict and otherworldly customs, like Buddhism and Hinduism. In the West, it has acquired ubiquity as a mainstream practice for pressure decrease, unwinding, and self-awareness.

Contemplation rehearses differ generally, with strategies going from care reflection, which underlines non-critical consciousness of the current second, to supernatural contemplation, which includes the utilization of a mantra to calm the psyche. In spite of these distinctions, many types of contemplation share normal consequences for cognizance. Ordinary contemplation practice has been related with expanded concentration and consideration, decreased nervousness and gloom, and upgrades in generally prosperity. The logical investigation of contemplation has given important experiences into the brain and mental systems fundamental these impacts.

Entrancing is one more charming changed condition of cognizance. It is a condition of centered consideration and elevated suggestibility, frequently joined by a sensation of profound unwinding. During spellbinding, people become more open to the ideas of a hypnotherapist, which can go from help with discomfort to memory review. Spellbinding has been utilized for restorative purposes, however it likewise conveys a long history of suspicion and discussion.

The exact idea of entrancing and its instruments stay a subject of discussion. A few scientists contend that entrancing includes a particular condition of cognizance, while others accept it is a blend of idea and pretending. In spite of these discussions, entrancing has been utilized effectively in clinical settings for torment the board, lessening tension, and treating specific mental circumstances.

One more unmistakable classification of adjusted conditions of cognizance is the utilization of psychoactive substances. Medications and synthetic substances can decisively adjust a singular's insight, discernment, and close to home state, prompting encounters that can be significantly not the same as conventional waking cognizance. The utilization of psychoactive substances has been an essential part of mankind's set of experiences, with substances like liquor, weed, and psychedelic drugs being consumed for different purposes, including strict customs, diversion, and self-investigation.

Psychedelic drugs, specifically, have drawn in impressive interest because of their ability to actuate significant modifications in discernment. Substances like LSD, psilocybin, and DMT can prompt encounters described by striking pipedreams, modified feeling of time, and a significant feeling of interconnectedness with the universe. Examination into the restorative capability of these substances, especially in the treatment of psychological wellness issues, has picked up speed lately.

The investigation of changed conditions of cognizance, including those initiated by psychoactive substances, has incited examinations concerning the fundamental neurological instruments. It is presently deep rooted that different substances can cooperate with the cerebrum's synapse frameworks, prompting changes in discernment, state of mind, and comprehension. The investigation of these substances and their belongings has added to how we might interpret cerebrum capability and can possibly illuminate the improvement regarding new medicines for emotional well-being issues.

Notwithstanding the individual and mental components of modified conditions of cognizance, there is a rich social and anthropological setting that encompasses these encounters. Various societies and social orders have created remarkable practices, customs, and convictions connected with modified states. These social varieties feature the variety of human encounters and the manners by which changed states are incorporated into the structure holding the system together.

In numerous native societies, modified conditions of cognizance assume a focal part in strict and shamanic rehearses. Plant medications like ayahuasca in the Amazon or peyote among Local American clans are utilized to actuate changed states that are accepted to associate people with the soul world, give recuperating, and offer experiences into the idea of presence. These practices are in many cases well established in custom and are viewed as fundamental for keeping up with social personality and profound prosperity.

The utilization of changed states with regards to strict and otherworldly practices isn't restricted to native societies. Over the entire course of time, different strict practices have utilized adjusted states to work with otherworldly encounters and experiences with the heavenly. For instance, in Sufi Islam, experts participate in spinning moves and reciting to prompt a daze like state, while in specific Christian groups, talking in tongues or different types of happy love are utilized to community with the Essence of God.

In the advanced Western world, the connection between modified states and otherworldliness has developed in different ways. A few people use contemplation and care rehearses for of investigating their internal identities and developing a feeling of otherworldly association. Others go to hallucinogenics, for example, the supposed entheogens, for encounters that are seen as profoundly otherworldly or supernatural. The crossing point of modified states and otherworldliness in contemporary culture is a complex and developing peculiarity, impacted by a scope of elements, including individual convictions, logical examination, and changing cultural perspectives.

7.1 Meditation, psychedelics, and shamanic practices

The investigation of modified conditions of cognizance has been a major part of mankind's set of experiences and culture. Among the different strategies and practices used to accomplish these modified states, reflection, hallucinogenics, and shamanic customs stand firm on noticeable situations. These methodologies offer one of a kind and significant bits of knowledge into the idea of human cognizance, otherworldliness, and the psyche's true capacity. In this thorough investigation, we dig into the unmistakable characteristics of reflection, hallucinogenics, and shamanic rehearses, every one of which gives a particular road to the investigation of changed states and their suggestions.

Reflection:

Reflection, a training that has been embraced by societies overall for millennia, is a focused way to deal with changing one's condition of cognizance. It includes centered consideration, frequently fixated on a particular article, thought, or sensation, fully intent on accomplishing an upgraded condition of mindfulness and inward peacefulness. The objectives of reflection change across customs, yet normal subjects incorporate lessening pressure, improving mindfulness, and arriving at a condition of mental quiet and lucidity.

One of the most generally perceived types of reflection is care contemplation. It gets from Buddhist practices and has been adjusted into mainstream and remedial settings. Care reflection urges the specialist to develop non-critical consciousness of the current second. This training includes noticing considerations, feelings, and sensations as they emerge without connection or revultion. The point is to foster a profound comprehension of one's psychological cycles and the capacity to be completely present in every second.

One more reflection practice with a rich history is supernatural contemplation (TM), which has acquired notoriety in the West. TM includes the reiteration of a particular mantra while keeping a latent demeanor, permitting contemplations to go back and forth without connection. The mantra fills in as a point of convergence for the psyche, assisting with calming mental gab and access a more profound condition of cognizance.

Contemplation's consequences for the psyche and body have been the subject of broad examination. Studies have demonstrated the way that normal contemplation practice can prompt upgrades in different parts of prosperity, including expanded consideration and fixation, diminished tension and discouragement, and improved profound guideline. Contemplation likewise has actual advantages, for example, decreasing pulse and further developing rest quality.

The instruments hidden these impacts are not completely perceived, however research recommends that contemplation might impact cerebrum design and capability. For instance, studies have shown changes in cerebrum locales related with consideration and close to home guideline in people who practice contemplation routinely.

These discoveries highlight the astounding versatility of the human cerebrum and its ability to adjust in light of centered mental preparation.

Besides, reflection isn't just a mental device yet additionally a profound practice in numerous customs. For example, in Hinduism and Buddhism, contemplation is a method for accomplishing edification and understanding one's real essence. It is accepted to be a way to greatness and a method for freeing oneself from the experiencing inborn in human life.

Hallucinogenics:

Hallucinogenic substances have spellbound human interest for quite a long time, offering a road to investigate changed conditions of cognizance that rise above standard insight and thought. Hallucinogenics, like LSD (lysergic corrosive diethylamide), psilocybin (the dynamic compound in enchantment mushrooms), and DMT (dimethyltryptamine), actuate significant adjustments in discernment, cognizance, and close to home insight. The impacts of hallucinogenics can go from uplifted tangible discernment and fantasies to significant experiences into the idea of presence.

The utilization of hallucinogenics has a long history, with native societies utilizing these substances in strict and shamanic customs. The Amazonian blend ayahuasca, for instance, has been involved by native networks in South America for quite a long time to speak with spirits and gain recuperating and knowledge. Essentially, peyote has been used by Local American clans in their profound practices.

During the twentieth 100 years, hallucinogenics acquired consideration in Western culture and were embraced by a nonconformity development looking for extended cognizance and self-revelation. This period saw crafted by figures like Timothy Leary, who broadly asked individuals to "turn on, tune in, nonconformist," advancing the utilization of hallucinogenics to rise above cultural standards and investigate the profundities of the human brain.

Contemporary examination into hallucinogenics has reignited interest in their possible helpful advantages. Studies have shown that hallucinogenics can be compelling in treating different psychological wellness conditions, including sadness, nervousness, and post-awful pressure issue. The instruments hidden these remedial impacts stay a subject of progressing research, yet it is accepted that hallucinogenics may prompt significant otherworldly or extraordinary encounters that can prompt individual experiences and close to home mending.

Neuroscientific examinations concerning hallucinogenics have exhibited that these substances cooperate with the mind's serotonin receptors, prompting adjustments in brain network and the arrival of synapses. These progressions are remembered to underlie the changed insights and cognizance experienced during a hallucinogenic outing. The investigation of hallucinogenics has extended how we might interpret cognizance as well as given new roads to investigating the mind's ability for change and recuperating.

The utilization of hallucinogenics, be that as it may, isn't without chances. These substances can prompt unfriendly impacts, for example, fits of anxiety, maniacal episodes, and testing encounters that some allude to as "terrible excursions." Improper use or an unacceptable setting can compound these dangers. Subsequently, there is a continuous discussion about the mindful and helpful utilization of hallucinogenics and the requirement for guideline to guarantee wellbeing.

Shamanic Practices:

Shamanic rehearses play had a crucial impact in native societies and address a novel way to deal with changing conditions of cognizance. Shamans are otherworldly pioneers and healers who are accepted to can speak with the soul world and access stowed away domains of the real world. Shamanic rehearses are well established in custom and are fundamental for keeping up with social character and otherworldly prosperity in numerous native social orders.

One of the center components of shamanic rehearses is the utilization of plant meds, which initiate adjusted conditions of cognizance that empower correspondence with the soul world. These plant meds, for example, ayahuasca in the Amazon, are key to shamanic ceremonies. They are consumed for of acquiring bits of knowledge, getting recuperating, and interfacing with familial spirits.

Shamanic travels frequently include a course of entering a daze state, which can be initiated through reciting, drumming, and moving. In this changed express, the shaman is accepted to go to the soul world, where they can recover lost spirits, give mending, and gain direction from hereditary spirits. These practices are helpful as well as act for of figuring out the interconnectedness of all life and the otherworldly elements of presence.

Shamanic rehearses are a demonstration of the significant and groundbreaking encounters that can be accomplished through changed conditions of cognizance. They offer a one of a kind point of view on the connection among people and the normal world, featuring the job of the shaman as a middle person between the physical and otherworldly domains.

The Cutting edge Convergence:

In present day times, the convergence of contemplation, hallucinogenics, and shamanic rehearses has led to a captivating juncture of thoughts and practices. While every one of these ways to deal with changed states has its particular qualities and objectives, they share normal subjects of self-revelation, otherworldly investigation, and the mission for a more profound comprehension of the brain.

Hallucinogenics and reflection, for example, have been united in ongoing exploration investigating the helpful capability of hallucinogenics. A few examinations have shown that people who have standard reflection practices might have more certain and reasonable encounters with hallucinogenics. Reflection's capacity to upgrade care and advance mindfulness might assume a part in relieving the likely difficulties of a hallucinogenic excursion.

Moreover, the convergence of shamanic rehearses and hallucinogenics has ignited a developing interest in the utilization of plant medications, as ayahuasca, beyond native settings. Retreat focuses and specialists in Western nations presently offer encounters with plant drugs for of otherworldly investigation, recuperating, and self-awareness. Nonetheless, this has raised worries about social appointment and the moral utilization of these substances.

What's more, there is continuous examination into the utilization of hallucinogenics in mix with contemplation and care rehearses. A few people have revealed that the utilization of hallucinogenics can improve their contemplation encounters, prompting further conditions of mindfulness and knowledge. Nonetheless, this area of study is still in its beginning phases, and more examination is expected to comprehend the possible advantages and dangers of this mix completely.

The investigation of modified conditions of cognizance stays a dynamic and developing field. The cooperative energy of contemplation, hallucinogenics, and shamanic rehearses keeps on giving new experiences into the idea of human awareness and the psyche's ability for change and mending. As logical exploration grows, and cultural mentalities develop, it is fundamental to explore this landscape with a decent point of view, perceiving both the likely advantages and dangers of these practices and regarding their social and individual variety.

7.2 Encounters with parallel dimensions

The idea of equal aspects, otherwise called equal universes or substitute real factors, has for some time been a subject of interest, hypothesis, and logical investigation. The possibility that there might exist different universes, comparable or incomprehensibly not quite the same as our own, has caught the human creative mind for a really long time. In this investigation, we dive into the idea of equal aspects, their authentic and philosophical roots, the logical speculations that help their reality, and the charming prospects of experiencing these substitute real factors.

Equal Aspects in History and Reasoning:

The thought of equal aspects has profound authentic and philosophical roots. All through mankind's set of experiences, societies have made stories and convictions that recommend the presence of numerous universes or domains past our regular experience. These equal aspects frequently appear as legendary or strict records, where divine beings, spirits, and extraordinary creatures possess substitute domains.

In old Greek way of thinking, for example, the possibility of the "Dispassionate domain" suggested that theoretical ideas, like equity or excellence, existed in a non-material, higher-layered domain. These philosophical thoughts laid the basis for contemplating aspects past the actual world.

Likewise, different strict customs and creation legends depict substitute domains or eminent aspects possessed by divine elements. In Christianity, the idea of paradise and damnation presents equal aspects that are particular from our natural presence. These profound aspects are in many cases portrayed as everlasting and outside human ability to understand.

In Eastern religions like Hinduism and Buddhism, the faith in resurrection recommends that the spirit can change between various aspects or domains in light of one's activities and karma. These domains, going from sublime heavens to appalling domains, address various components of presence.

Equal aspects stretches out into fables and legends. Across various societies, accounts of entryways or passages to different universes flourish. These gateways, whether concealed in the profundities of a woodland or on an otherworldly mountain, act as points of admittance to substitute aspects loaded up with enchanted animals, difficulties, and marvels.

Equal Aspects in Present day Material science:

While equal aspects have profound verifiable and philosophical roots, they certainly stand out enough to be noticed of present day physical science. The idea of equal aspects is a characteristic expansion of speculations in material science that try to make sense of the central idea of the universe. Speculations that help the presence of equal aspects, like string hypothesis and the multiverse speculation, address the front line of logical investigation.

String Hypothesis: One of the most unmistakable speculations proposing the presence of equal aspects is string hypothesis. String hypothesis sets that the central structure blocks of the universe are not particles but rather small, vibrating strings. These strings exist in higher-layered spaces past our typical three spatial aspects and once aspect.

String hypothesis recommends that there might be extra secret aspects, past the natural three elements of room. These additional aspects could be compactified or "nestled into" firmly that they are vague to us on perceptible scales. In any case, they may as yet impact the central powers and particles of the universe.

The ramifications of string hypothesis are significant. In the event that these additional aspects exist, they could give a system to understanding key powers like gravity and the connections between particles. Moreover, string hypothesis raises the chance of a "scene" of various arrangements, addressing different universes or aspects with various actual properties.

Multiverse Speculation: The multiverse speculation takes equal aspects much further. It proposes the presence of a couple of equal aspects as well as a whole multiverse — a huge assortment of universes, each with its own arrangement of actual regulations, constants, and conditions. This idea challenges our conventional thought of a solitary, one of a kind universe.

The multiverse speculation comes in a few structures. In the "many-universes" translation of quantum mechanics, for example, each conceivable quantum result is acknowledged in a different part of the universe. Inflationary cosmology proposes that our universe is only one of many air pocket universes that persistently swell inside a bigger grandiose scene.

These hypotheses have ignited an entrancing discussion inside established researchers. While they offer answers for a few well established issues in material science, they likewise present difficulties concerning observational proof and testability. The thought of equal aspects, in this specific situation, stays a hypothetical develop, but a captivating one.

Potential Entrances to Resemble Aspects:

Assuming equal aspects exist, the regular inquiry emerges: How should one experience or connect with them? While quite a bit of this stays theoretical, different peculiarities, both regular and human-made, have been proposed as expected gateways or roads to get to resemble aspects.

Wormholes: Wormholes are hypothetical passages or easy routes in spacetime that could associate far off locales of the universe. Anticipated by Einstein's hypothesis of general relativity, wormholes are similar to spans between various locales of spacetime. On the off chance that steady and safe, wormholes could act as entries to different aspects or even far off pieces of our own universe.

The idea of wormholes has caught the public's creative mind and has been a staple in sci-fi. While they remain simply hypothetical at this stage, they are predictable with the science of general relativity. Their reality, in any case, is dependent upon the presence of fascinating types of issue with negative energy thickness, which has not yet been noticed.

Quantum Snare: Quantum ensnarement is a peculiarity in quantum physical science where at least two particles become connected so that the condition of one molecule is connected to the condition of another, no matter what the distance between them. This peculiarity is frequently portrayed as "creepy activity a ways off" by Einstein.

A few physicists have conjectured that quantum snare could be bridled to lay out correspondence or associations between particles in various aspects or equal universes. This thought remains exceptionally speculative, and the reasonable difficulties of taking advantage of quantum trap for such objects are impressive.

Grandiose Strings: Astronomical strings are speculative one-layered objects that might exist in the texture of spacetime. These strings are a result of specific hypotheses in cosmology and could make districts of concentrated energy or "wrinkles" in space-time. It has been recommended that these crimps could act as entryways to different aspects.

The possibility of infinite strings as entrances stays speculative and is right now a subject of examination and discussion inside established researchers. While vast strings have not been straightforwardly noticed, their likely ramifications for how we might interpret the universe are interesting.

Human Cognizance and Modified States: A few scholars suggest that human awareness might hold the way to experiencing equal aspects. Certain modified conditions of cognizance, like those instigated through reflection, hallucinogenic substances, or profound conditions of unwinding, are accepted to give an entryway to different domains of presence.

In this point of view, cognizance is viewed as a non-neighborhood peculiarity that can rise above the limits of normal reality. Through modified states, people might have the option to get to substitute aspects or see real factors past their common tangible discernments. This idea repeats the possibility of shamanic rehearses, where adjusted states work with correspondence with the soul world or substitute real factors.

Experiences with Equal Aspects: Fiction and Hypothesis:
While the logical comprehension of equal aspects stays in its beginning phases, experiences with substitute real factors have been a common subject in writing, craftsmanship, and mainstream society. Sci-fi and speculative fiction have long investigated getting over into equal aspects, frequently with intriguing and inventive outcomes.

In writing, the idea of equal aspects has been a rich wellspring of narrating. Creators like H.G. Wells, in his book "The Time Machine," and Philip K. Dick, in works like "The Man in the High Palace" and "Ubik," have portrayed characters who cross substitute real factors or wrestle with equal aspects. These stories bring up issues about the idea of the real world, personality, and the results of decisions.

Equal aspects have likewise been highlighted unmistakably in TV and film. The TV series "Periphery" investigates equal universes and the outcomes of associations between them. The "Sliders" series spins around characters who travel to various equal Earths through an entrance. Such portrayals spellbind crowds by permitting them to really pause for a moment to think about the significant potential outcomes and difficulties of experiencing substitute real factors.

In speculative and philosophical idea, the idea of equal aspects brings up significant issues about the idea of the real world, cognizance, and presence. It challenges how we might interpret oneself, recommending that numerous variants of an individual could exist across various aspects, each going with various decisions and having particular existences. Equal aspects likewise prompts reflections on the idea of causality, destiny, and choice.

The philosophical ramifications of equal aspects venture into conversations about the idea of reality itself. In the event that equal aspects exist, they brief investigations into the idea of presence, the potential for various real factors coinciding, and the interconnecte.

7.3 Expanding the boundaries of human awareness

The mission to grow the limits of human mindfulness has been a crucial main impetus all through mankind's set of experiences. This undertaking, established in our natural interest and hunger for information, has prompted momentous advances in different fields, including science, innovation, theory, and otherworldliness. In this investigation, we dig into the multi-layered manners by which people have looked to rise above their present status of mindfulness and arrive at new degrees of understanding, both of themselves and the universe.

The Quest for Information and Science:

One of the essential manners by which people have extended their mindfulness is through the quest for information and the logical technique. From the earliest perceptions of the normal world to contemporary logical exploration, the method involved with looking for replies to essential inquiries has been a main impetus behind human advancement.

The logical technique, with its accentuation on exact perception, speculation testing, and the aggregation of proof, has upset how we might interpret the actual world. It has permitted us to investigate the microcosm of subatomic particles, the immeasurability of the universe, and the complexities of life itself. Logical disclosures have extended our familiarity with the universe's age, structure, and actual regulations, prompting a more profound comprehension of the universe.

Progressions in fields like stargazing, material science, science, and neuroscience have given significant experiences into the idea of the real world. For instance, the hypothesis of relativity, created by Albert Einstein, has in a general sense changed our understanding of room, time, and gravity. The disclosure of the design of DNA by James Watson and Francis Cramp has enlightened the instruments hidden life itself.

The mission for information reaches out past the actual sciences to envelop the social and conduct sciences. Brain science, social science, and humanities try to grasp the intricacies of human way of behaving, insight, and culture. These disciplines have extended our consciousness of the human brain, society, and our place inside the multifaceted snare of human collaboration.

In ongoing many years, the investigation of cognizance has acquired noticeable quality as a multidisciplinary try. Specialists from different fields, including brain research, neuroscience, and reasoning, are examining the idea of cognizance, emotional experience, and the brain processes basic mindfulness. This crossing point of logical disciplines plans to push the limits of human mindfulness by interpreting the mystery of the psyche.

Innovative Progressions:
Mechanical developments play had a significant impact in extending the limits of human mindfulness. Since the beginning of time, people have outfit innovation to rise above their organic limits and arrive at new degrees of understanding.

The improvement of telescopes, for example, has empowered stargazers to investigate the universe for a great scope. Galileo's utilization of a telescope in the seventeenth century upset our view of the universe by uncovering the moons of Jupiter and the periods of Venus. Ensuing advances in adjustable innovation have permitted us to notice far off systems, stars, and planets, revealing insight into the immeasurability of the universe.

Also, the magnifying instrument has disclosed the secret universe of microorganisms and cells, changing comprehension we might interpret science. Tiny innovation has worked with leap forwards in the investigation of irresistible sicknesses, hereditary qualities, and the complexities of life at the cell level.

In the domain of correspondence, the advancement of the web has interconnected the world in extraordinary ways. The advanced age has extended our mindfulness by giving admittance to immense vaults of information, cultivating worldwide correspondence, and empowering the quick scattering of data. The web has catalyzed logical coordinated effort, worked with instructive open doors, and opened up new roads for sharing different viewpoints and encounters.

Headways in imaging advances, for example, attractive reverberation imaging (X-ray) and practical X-ray (fMRI), have permitted us to investigate the complexities of the human mind and its part in cognizance. These innovations have given bits of knowledge into mind capability, offering a brief look into the brain underpinnings of insight, memory, and feelings.

Computer generated reality (VR) and increased reality (AR) innovations can possibly additionally grow the limits of human mindfulness. By submerging people in mimicked conditions or overlaying computerized data onto the actual world, VR and

AR have the ability to change the manner in which we learn, see our environmental factors, and experience substitute real factors.

Moreover, the improvement of man-made reasoning (artificial intelligence) and AI can possibly upgrade our mindfulness in different areas. Computer based intelligence frameworks can deal with immense measures of information, perceive examples, and make expectations, supporting analysts in fields as different as environment science, clinical diagnostics, and molecule physical science.

Philosophical and Magical Investigations:

Extending the limits of human mindfulness isn't exclusively the space of science and innovation. Reasoning and mysticism have long looked to wrestle with significant inquiries regarding the idea of the real world, oneself, and the universe.

From the beginning of time, savants have investigated the ideas of the real world, discernment, and awareness. The old Greeks, for instance, took part in banters about the idea of the real world, with masterminds like Plato proposing the presence of a higher domain of ideal structures. Aristotle dove into the way of thinking of psyche and discernment, establishing the groundwork for conversations about the idea of mindfulness.

In Eastern way of thinking, customs like Buddhism and Hinduism have dove into the idea of awareness and oneself. The idea of illumination, as sought after in these practices, addresses the development of mindfulness and the greatness of egoic limits.

Otherworldly investigations, for example, those tracked down in magical practices, mean to go outside regular ability to grasp and accomplish immediate, extraordinary encounters. Spiritualists from different practices have depicted significant conditions of cognizance that oppose conventional discernment. These encounters frequently include a feeling of solidarity, unity, and association with the universe.

Existential way of thinking, as exemplified by crafted by Jean-Paul Sartre and Albert Camus, wrestles with inquiries of presence, opportunity, and the quest for importance. The existentialist viewpoint urges people to face the limits of their own reality and mindfulness, frequently prompting a more profound assessment of one's life and decisions.

The prospering field of reasoning of brain, which investigates the idea of cognizance, deliberateness, and the psyche body issue, looks to grow how we might interpret mindfulness. Thinkers in this field examine the connection between mental peculiarities and the actual world, pushing the limits of human comprehension of the psyche.

Otherworldly and Magical Pursuits:

Profound and magical customs from around the world have long sought after the extension of human mindfulness through rehearses that rise above the standard domain of insight. These practices frequently stress direct private experience, frequently depicted as supernatural or otherworldly conditions of awareness.

Reflection is a foundation of numerous otherworldly works on, permitting people to investigate changed conditions of cognizance and arrive at more profound degrees of mindfulness. Rehearses like care reflection, Harmony contemplation, and supernatural reflection are intended to develop an increased condition of presence and mindfulness.

Yoga, starting from old Indian customs, includes actual stances, breath control, and contemplation to extend cognizance and achieve profound arousing. Yoga professionals expect to join the body, brain, and soul, rising above the impediments of common mindfulness.

The utilization of hallucinogenic substances, for example, ayahuasca and psilocybin-containing mushrooms, has been fundamental to shamanic and native profound practices. These substances are accepted to work with direct correspondence with the soul world, prompting significant experiences, mending, and change. Hallucinogenic encounters can possibly grow human mindfulness by giving admittance to substitute real factors and aspects.

Different types of blissful or magical encounters are accounted for across strict practices. In Christianity, spiritualists like St. John of the Cross and St. Teresa of Ávila have portrayed serious experiences with the heavenly. Sufi Islam consolidates rehearses like spinning dervishes and reciting to prompt otherworldly conditions of cognizance. In Hinduism, fans of the Bhakti development look for an immediate, cherishing relationship with the heavenly, growing their mindfulness through commitment and give up.

Contemporary otherworldly developments, like the New Age development and transpersonal brain science, underscore the investigation of higher conditions of cognizance and extended mindfulness. These developments frequently draw from various customs and works on, empowering people to look for individual change and a more profound association with the universe.

Experiences with Extended Territories of Mindfulness:

Experiences with extended conditions of mindfulness can appear in different ways, each giving extraordinary bits of knowledge and encounters. These experiences might result from logical investigation, mechanical progression, philosophical request, or profound practices. They frequently challenge our assumptions, grow how we might interpret reality, and deal significant looks into the secrets of presence.

Logical investigation and leap forwards can prompt outlook changes in human mindfulness. The hypothesis of relativity, for instance, changed how we might interpret spacetime and gravity. The disclosure of quantum mechanics tested our regular perspective on particles and their way of behaving at the subatomic.

Chapter 8

The Multiverse in Literature and Art

The idea of the multiverse has been a captivating and provocative subject in writing and craftsmanship for a long time. An idea extends the limits of our creative mind and difficulties how we might interpret reality. In this investigation, we will dig into the different manners by which the multiverse has been portrayed, investigated, and analyzed in the domains of writing and workmanship.

At its center, the multiverse is a hypothetical system that places the presence of numerous universes or equal real factors coinciding close by our own. This thought has its underlying foundations in logical hypotheses, especially in quantum physical science, yet it has likewise tracked down prolific ground in the imaginative personalities of journalists and craftsmen. The idea of substitute real factors and equal universes considers vast conceivable outcomes, and it has been utilized to investigate a great many subjects, from the idea of the real world and personality to the results of our decisions.

One of the earliest cases of the multiverse in writing can be followed back to the nineteenth hundred years. In Lewis Carroll's "Into another world," the continuation of "Alice's Experiences in Wonderland," Alice ventures through a mirror and regards herself as in an equal world, where everything is switched. This fantastical domain is a forerunner to imaginary worlds, where the principles of the truth are unique in relation to our own. Carroll's work established the groundwork for future investigations of the multiverse in writing.

As the twentieth century unfolded, the idea of the multiverse acquired much more noticeable quality in sci-fi. H.G. Wells, one of the trailblazers of the class, dug into equal universes in his 1931 book "The Entryway in the Wall." In this story, a man experiences a baffling green entryway that transports him to an alternate reality where he carries on with an alternate existence. Wells' investigation of the multiverse was not restricted to sci-fi, as he involved it as an instrument to inspect subjects of decision and lament.

Equal universes and substitute real factors kept on charming journalists and perusers all through the twentieth 100 years. In 1962, Philip K. Dick's book "The Man in the High Palace" portrayed a substitute history in which the Pivot powers had won The Second Great War. The clever investigated the results of such a reality and scrutinized the idea of truth and discernment. Dick's work was a huge achievement in the investigation of the multiverse in writing and presented the idea of "consider the possibility that" situations.

Sci-fi has been a rich ground for the multiverse idea, with creators like Isaac Asimov, Arthur C. Clarke, and Robert A. Heinlein integrating it into their accounts. In Asimov's "The Finish of Endlessness," a time-travel association that can modify history investigates the effect of changes in substitute real factors. Clarke's "The City and the Stars" happens in a far-future Earth with a strange past, alluding to various patterns of progress. Heinlein's "The Quantity of the Monster" includes a machine that can cross equal universes, permitting the characters to investigate different fictitious and verifiable universes.

The multiverse idea in writing isn't bound to sci-fi alone. It has likewise shown up in standard and abstract fiction. In Kurt Vonnegut's "Slaughterhouse-Five," the hero Billy Pioneer becomes "unstuck in time," encountering minutes from his life out of arrangement. This story structure obscures the limits between various minutes in time, making a feeling of different real factors. Vonnegut's work difficulties conventional thoughts of linearity in narrating.

The investigation of the multiverse isn't restricted to the composed word; it has likewise been a common subject in visual craftsmanship. Craftsmen have utilized different mediums to portray the idea of various real factors, frequently obscuring the line between the genuine and the envisioned. Oddity, specifically, has been a fruitful ground for such investigation. Specialists like Salvador Dali and Rene Magritte made illusory, extraordinary scenes that challenge our view of the real world.

Dali's well known painting "The Steadiness of Memory" highlights softening tickers and an infertile scene, summoning a feeling of immortality and twisting of the real world. Magritte's "The Foul play of Pictures" gives a line the subtitle, "Ceci n'est pas une pipe" (This isn't a line), featuring the difference between an item and its portrayal. These show-stoppers welcome watchers to scrutinize the idea of the real world and portrayal.

In the domain of contemporary craftsmanship, the multiverse keeps on being a wellspring of motivation. Advanced workmanship and computer generated reality have opened up additional opportunities for craftsmen to make vivid encounters that transport watchers to substitute real factors. Specialists like Yayoi Kusama have utilized reflected rooms and limitlessness nets to make the deception of endless space, welcoming watchers to ponder the possibility of an unlimited multiverse.

The idea of the multiverse has likewise tracked down a home in the realm of film and TV. From mind-bowing sci-fi movies to provocative shows, equal universes has been a common subject in visual narrating. Christopher Nolan's "Commencement" investigates the idea of settled dreams, where each level of the fantasy land is a different reality. The film provokes the characters and the crowd to recognize dream and reality.

TV series like "A Twilight Zone" and "The X-Records" have dug into the multiverse, frequently introducing independent episodes that investigate substitute real factors and the unexplored world. "A Twilight Zone" is especially renowned for its moral and philosophical stories set in equal universes, where characters should wrestle with the outcomes of their decisions.

The Wonder True to life Universe (MCU) has additionally embraced the multiverse, with films like "Specialist Odd" and the Disney+ series "Loki" presenting stretching timetables and substitute real factors. The MCU's investigation of the multiverse has opened up new narrating prospects, permitting characters to communicate with their substitute selves and return to enter minutes previously.

While the multiverse idea is an integral asset for narrating, it likewise fills in for of investigating complex philosophical and powerful inquiries. It challenges how we might interpret reality, character, and the idea of presence. It requests us to consider the ramifications from our decisions and the possibility that there might be boundless adaptations of ourselves in equal universes, each settling on various choices and carrying on with various existences.

The multiverse likewise proposes a novel viewpoint on the suggestion of destiny and through and through freedom. In the event that there are endless substitute real factors, each with its own arrangement of decisions and results, do our choices genuinely matter? Or then again would we say we are essentially one of numerous emphasess of ourselves in a boundless ocean of potential outcomes? This existential addressing is a common subject in writing and craftsmanship that brings us into a philosophical thought of our spot in the universe.

In writing, writers like Jorge Luis Borges have utilized the multiverse to investigate the idea of endlessness and the restrictions of human information. In his story "The Library of Babel," Borges envisions a huge and boundless library containing each conceivable book that can be composed. This allegorical library brings up issues about the idea of truth, information, and the vanity of looking for significance in a limitless and vast universe.

The idea of the multiverse likewise has significant ramifications for how we might interpret individual character. Assuming there are limitless forms of ourselves in equal universes, each with its own encounters and decisions, what's the significance here to be "me"? This question is at the core of works as moorcock Michael's "The Timeless Boss" series, where the hero is resurrected in various universes, each with an alternate fate and personality.

In craftsmanship, the multiverse challenges our view of room, time, and reality. Specialists like M.C. Escher have made perplexing, mind-bowing visual riddles that play with ideas of endlessness and Catch 22. Escher's well known lithograph

"Relativity" portrays a reality where gravity appears to act every which way, making a maze of flights of stairs that challenge the laws of material science.

The multiverse likewise welcomes us to scrutinize the limits between the cognizant and the inner mind. Surrealist craftsmen like Andre Breton and Max Ernst have utilized fanciful symbolism to investigate the secret domains of the psyche. Their works frequently obscure the line between the genuine and the dreamlike, welcoming watchers to mull over the interconnectedness of internal and external universes.

The investigation of the multiverse in writing and workmanship isn't restricted to Western culture. Many societies all over the planet have their own legends and stories that touch upon the possibility of numerous real factors. In Hindu folklore, for instance, the idea of "Lila" recommends that the universe is a vast play, with endless divine beings and goddesses making and obliterating universes in a timeless cycle. This point of view difficulties the possibility of a solitary, straight reality and supports a more liquid comprehension of presence.

The multiverse idea has likewise been embraced by contemporary sci-fi scholars, who attract motivation from state of the art speculations physical science and cosmology. The field of quantum mechanics, specifically, has given a hypothetical structure to the presence of equal universes. The popular Schrödinger's feline psychological test, wherein a feline is both alive and dead until noticed, represents the idea of superposition, where particles can exist in various states all the while. This thought has prompted speculations about expanding courses of events and substitute real factors.

8.1 Science fiction narratives and the multiverse

Sci-fi has for quite some time been a class that welcomes investigation of the obscure, the speculative, and the strange regions of human creative mind. Inside the tremendous breadth of sci-fi writing and media, one repeating and spellbinding subject has been the idea of the multiverse. The multiverse, a hypothetical system drawn from physical science and reasoning, places the presence of various universes or equal real factors, each with its own novel arrangement of conditions, conceivable outcomes, and results. In this paper, we will dig into the diverse manners by which sci-fi accounts have embraced and used the idea of the multiverse, taking perusers and watchers on ventures through substitute aspects, unique timetables, and equal universes.

The investigation of the multiverse in sci-fi isn't just a practice in idealism or unadulterated dream. All things considered, it fills in as an amazing asset for journalists and makers to wrestle with complex philosophical and existential inquiries. The multiverse welcomes us to think about the idea of the real world, the effect of decisions and choices, the idea of individual personality, and the transaction of destiny and freedom of thought. It additionally challenges how we might interpret the universe and its major properties, taking into account inventive and speculative understandings of the universe.

One of the original works in sci-fi writing that presented the idea of the multiverse to a more extensive crowd is H.G. Wells' "The Conflict of the Universes." In this

1898 novel, the hero experiences Martians attacking Earth, opening up the chance of extraterrestrial life. The story alludes to the presence of other occupied planets and, likewise, the possibility of different universes past our own. Wells' work may not unequivocally dive into the hypothetical parts of the multiverse, however it makes way for the investigation of elective real factors and the presence of powerful creatures.

The twentieth century saw a multiplication of sci-fi stories that dove into the multiverse, especially following advances in quantum physical science and hypothetical cosmology. These stories frequently challenge our customary comprehension of the real world, time, and space, welcoming perusers and watchers to mull over the significant ramifications of a multiverse structure.

In 1956, Philip K. Dick's "The Minority Report" presented an existence where mystics can foresee violations before they happen, considering preplanned captures. The story investigates the possibility of determinism and unrestrained choice as well as the results of knowing what's to come. While the account doesn't expressly include equal universes, it brings up issues about the idea of decision and the chance of dissimilar ways such one's reality could take in light of various choices.

An original work in the investigation of the multiverse in sci-fi is Robert A. Heinlein's 1957 book "The Entryway into Summer." This novel presents the idea of time travel and substitute real factors through the development of a "period entryway" that permits characters to go in reverse and forward in time. The hero, Dan Davis, sets out on an excursion through time and experiences numerous variants of himself in different real factors, each going with various decisions and encountering various results. Heinlein's work investigates the multiverse as well as dives into topics of affection, lament, and the idea of individual character.

The idea of spreading timetables and equal universes turned into a focal topic in sci-fi with the coming of the many-universes understanding of quantum mechanics. This understanding, proposed by physicist Hugh Everett III in 1957, places that each quantum occasion brings about the formation of numerous fanning universes, each comparing to an alternate result.

The many-universes understanding gave sci-fi creators a strong structure for investigating the multiverse and its suggestions.

One of the most notorious sci-fi series to embrace the multiverse idea is "Star Trip." Made by Quality Roddenberry, "Star Journey" includes a huge, different universe populated by various outsider species, each with its own way of life, history, and innovative progression. The establishment investigates topics of discretion, investigation, and moral situations, frequently through the experiences of various starship teams with substitute variants of the real world. The idea of equal universes is clearly depicted in the "Mirror Universe" episodes, where the characters experience partners who have settled on various moral decisions and possess a merciless, dictator system.

The "Star Trip" establishment likewise presented the idea of substitute real factors through time travel, frequently bringing about different courses of events. In "Star

Journey: The Future," the episode "Equals" sees the person Worf moving between numerous equal universes, each with its own adaptation of the Endeavor and its team. This investigation of the multiverse features the delicacy of the real world and the possibility that each choice or occasion can prompt an alternate result, a subject that resounds with the many-universes understanding of quantum mechanics.

Equal universes and substitute real factors have been repeating topics in writing also. Michael Moorcock's "The Timeless Boss" series, which started during the 1960s, follows the experiences of different manifestations of the Everlasting Hero, a legend who is resurrected in various universes. Every manifestation of the Top dog faces special difficulties and moral problems, featuring the complex idea of individual personality and predetermination. Moorcock's work brings up issues about the interconnectedness of all real factors and the recurrent idea of presence.

The investigation of the multiverse isn't restricted to composed writing and TV. Sci-fi films have additionally embraced the idea, offering crowds outwardly convincing excursions through substitute aspects and equal universes. Christopher Nolan's 2010 film "Commencement" is a perfect representation of how the multiverse can be woven into a story. The film spins around the idea of dream sharing and the capacity to enter different layers of dreams inside dreams. Each layer addresses an alternate reality with its own actual regulations and difficulties, obscuring the limits among dream and reality. "Commencement" provokes the characters and the crowd to recognize the different degrees of the real world and investigate the outcomes of decisions made inside those levels.

The 2014 movie "Edge of Tomorrow," coordinated by Doug Liman and in light of Hiroshi Sakurazaka's book "All You Really want Is Kill," includes a hero who becomes caught in a period circle, remembering that very day over and over. This account gadget permits the person to gain from every cycle and settle on various decisions, eventually influencing the course of occasions.

The film presents the possibility of disparate timetables and the expected for one person's activities to change the direction of a whole conflict. It fills in as a drawing in investigation of the multiverse idea inside the structure of a cutting edge, high-stakes fight.

The idea of the multiverse has additionally influenced the domain of TV. "Specialist Who," an English sci-fi series that has spread over many years, includes a time-traveling outsider known as the Specialist who can recover into various structures. The show investigates the idea of equal universes and substitute real factors through the "equal Earth" storyline, where the Specialist experiences substitute renditions of recognizable characters and investigates the results of various authentic occasions.

"The Blaze," a TV series in view of the DC Comic books character of a similar name, integrates the idea of the multiverse into its story. The show includes a "multiverse" comprising of equal Earths, each with its own interesting history and legends. Characters from one Earth sporadically get over into different Earths, prompting experiences with substitute adaptations of themselves and their partners. This account approach permits the show to investigate subjects of character, decision, and the interconnectedness of various real factors.

Sci-fi accounts have frequently utilized the multiverse to dive into philosophical and mystical inquiries. One of the focal subjects investigated through the multiverse is the idea of the real world. Assuming that there are innumerable substitute real factors, each with its own arrangement of conditions and conceivable outcomes, what characterizes the idea of "reality" itself? This question difficulties how we might interpret the universe and its basic properties. It welcomes us to consider the idea of presence and the degree to which our own existence is only one among many.

The multiverse additionally brings up significant issues about private personality. Assuming there are limitless forms of ourselves in equal universes, each going with various decisions and encountering various results, what's the significance here to be "me"? This question is at the core of numerous sci-fi stories that investigate the multiverse, for example, the previously mentioned "The Entryway into Summer" by Robert A. Heinlein. The idea of experiencing substitute adaptations of oneself in various real factors prompts characters and crowds to ponder the idea of distinction and the degree to which our decisions characterize what our identity is.

Besides, the multiverse welcomes us to scrutinize the exchange among destiny and freedom of thought. Assuming there are numerous universes, each with its own arrangement of occasions and results, which job does decision play in forming the course of one's life? Are our choices foreordained, or do they have the ability to change the direction of the real world? These inquiries have profound philosophical ramifications and have been investigated in sci-fi stories that draw in with the multiverse.

8.2 The concept of the "mirror universe"

The idea of the "reflect universe" has been a charming and persevering through subject in sci-fi. It fills in as a story gadget that investigates substitute real factors, equal universes, and the captivating thought that there are elective forms of characters and occasions. The mirror universe idea isn't restricted to a particular sci-fi establishment however has been embraced and adjusted by different creators, TV series, and producers. In this article, we will dig into the complex idea of the mirror universe, its advancement inside the sci-fi type, and its part in investigating topics of duality, ethical quality, and the outcomes of decisions.

The idea of the mirror universe frequently includes the making of an equal reality that is an identical representation of the essential or "prime" universe. In this other reality, characters and occasions might be modified or changed in huge ways, prompting a world that is frequently hazier, more merciless, and ethically unmistakable from the first universe. While the specific subtleties of the mirror universe might change starting with one work of sci-fi then onto the next, certain normal components characterize this story gadget.

One of the earliest and most famous instances of the mirror universe can be viewed as in the first "Star Journey" series. In the episode "Mirror, Mirror" from the subsequent season, individuals from the USS Endeavor team are coincidentally shipped to an equal universe where the Unified Organization of Planets is an overbearing Realm, and the group individuals are merciless and eager for power. The episode presented the idea of a "reflect" universe, a term that would become inseparable from substitute real factors in the "Star Trip" establishment.

The mirror universe in "Star Trip" investigates topics of duality and the effect of decisions and conditions on individual and aggregate profound quality. It presents a distinct difference to the recognizable universe of the Organization, where upsides of harmony, collaboration, and investigation win. In the mirror universe, characters frequently face moral situations that challenge their loyalties, and devotions are liquid. The episode "Mirror, Mirror" represents this ethical investigation as characters from the excellent universe are defied with the fierce idea of their mirror partners.

Throughout the long term, the mirror universe idea has turned into a common subject in "Star Trip," with ensuing series and episodes further creating and growing this substitute reality. The mirror universe has been highlighted in "Star Journey: Profound Space Nine," "Star Trip: Endeavor," and "Star Trip: Revelation," each offering novel experiences into the idea of this equal world. The mirror universe fills in as a provocative setting for investigating the outcomes of decisions and the smoothness of profound quality.

In "Star Trip: Profound Space Nine," the two-section episode "Hybrid" and "Into another world" offers a more profound investigation of the mirror universe. In these episodes, the station's team becomes entrapped with their mirror partners, prompting complex cooperations and battles for control. The mirror universe in "Profound Space Nine" is described by its anarchic and tumultuous nature, where coalitions are delicate, and treachery is ordinary. The episodes feature the subject of duality and the possibility that people's decisions can lead them down boundlessly various ways.

The mirror universe likewise permits "Star Journey" to undermine character models and investigate the hazier parts of recognizable characters. In the mirror universe, characters who are ordinarily temperate and moral might become savage and eager for power, while the people who are many times adversarial in the excellent universe might become impossible partners. This disruption challenges watchers' assumptions of character qualities and the possibility that people are innately great or wickedness, supporting the thought that conditions and decisions assume a critical part in forming one's personality.

"Star Journey: Endeavor" kept on extending the mirror universe story with the two-section episode "In a Mirror, Dimly." In this episode, the team of the USS Undertaking experiences a starship from the mirror universe and becomes entangled in a contention for power and endurance. "In a Mirror, Obscurely" offers a new viewpoint on the innovation and style of the mirror universe, mirroring the strategic and forceful nature of this equal reality.

"Star Trip: Revelation" brought the mirror universe into its subsequent season, where the team of the USS Disclosure coincidentally winds up in this substitute reality. The series investigates the idea of the mirror universe further, digging into its set of experiences and the explanations for the ethical dissimilarity from the excellent universe. "Disclosure" offers a more nuanced perspective on the mirror universe, uncovering that even in this brutal and unforgiving world, people can discover a feeling of profound quality and reclamation.

Past "Star Trip," the mirror universe idea has been embraced by other sci-fi establishments and creators. The "Periphery" TV series, made by J.J. Abrams, Alex Kurtzman, and Roberto Orci, presented an equal universe as a focal plot component. In this series, an equal universe exists close by the essential world, and the characters should explore the results of their activities in the two real factors. "Periphery" investigates the topic of interconnectedness between various universes and the effect of decisions on both the characters and the texture of the real world.

The idea of the mirror universe isn't restricted to the domain of TV yet has likewise advanced into sci-fi writing. Philip K. Dick's book "Counter-Clock World" offers a novel contort on the mirror universe idea. In this novel, time streams in reverse, and people come back to life, carrying on with their lives backward. The mirror universe in "Counter-Clock World" challenges the ordinary request of time and investigates subjects of life and demise, predetermination, and the outcomes of decisions.

The mirror universe idea, no matter what the particular story or establishment, fills in as a rich material for investigating the dualities of human instinct. It prompts us to scrutinize the idea of profound quality, the effect of decisions, and the smoothness of character. It challenges how we might interpret the deterministic and indeterministic parts of the real world and the degree to which people are formed by their conditions.

The mirror universe additionally brings up the issue of how people and social orders answer misfortune and brutal circumstances. In many mirror universe stories, characters wind up in fierce and unforgiving conditions, which can draw out the most exceedingly terrible or best in them. The mirror universe fills in as a critique on the flexibility of human way of behaving and the moral problems looked by people when set in outrageous circumstances.

Furthermore, the mirror universe frequently includes characters who are ethically vague, exploring an existence where coalitions are brief and treachery is a consistent danger. This ethical vagueness challenges the conventional thoughts of legends and lowlifes, it are intricate and complex to support the possibility that people. It welcomes watchers and perusers to scrutinize the idea of good and malicious and the limit with regards to reclamation and change.

The investigation of the mirror universe idea isn't restricted to ethical quality and character improvement. It likewise offers a special viewpoint on the outcomes of decisions and activities. In many mirror universe stories, characters should wrestle with the repercussions of their choices, both in the mirror universe and the superb universe. The mirror universe fills in as a wake up call, advising us that our decisions have broad impacts, and the ways we decide to follow can wander fundamentally from our expected objective.

Besides, the mirror universe idea welcomes us to consider the ramifications of an existence where moral standards and cultural designs are incomprehensibly not the same as those of the excellent universe. It urges us to consider the job of culture, climate, and childhood in forming individual and aggregate qualities. The mirror universe challenges how we might interpret how social orders are framed and the way in which they keep everything under control or bedlam.

The mirror universe idea has advanced throughout the long term, reflecting changes in cultural perspectives and the moving elements of narrating. While the first "Star Trip" episode "Mirror, Mirror" offered a conspicuous difference between the prime and mirror universes, resulting emphasess of the idea have presented more nuanced and complex stories. The mirror universe has turned into a story instrument for investigating the ill defined situations of profound quality and the interconnectedness of various real factors.

8.3 Parallel worlds in artistic expressions

Craftsmanship has for some time been a material for the investigation of substitute real factors and equal universes. Through different imaginative structures like writing, visual craftsmanship, film, and music, makers have moved crowds to substitute aspects, equal universes, and fantastical domains. These creative articulations frequently act as a way to get away from the bounds of the real world, challenge our discernments, and dive into the unfamiliar domains of human creative mind. In this investigation, we will dig into the diverse manners by which craftsmen across various mediums have embraced the idea of equal universes and the effect of these imaginative articulations on how we might interpret reality and innovativeness.

Writing: The Doorway to Resemble Universes

Writing has been an essential mode for the investigation of equal universes. Writers have utilized the composed word to make multifaceted and vivid domains that challenge how we might interpret reality and make the way for boundless conceivable outcomes. One of the earliest occurrences of equal universes in writing can be found in Lewis Carroll's "Alice's Undertakings in Wonderland." In this famous work, Alice enters a dark hole and ends up in a fantastical existence where rationale and the truth are overturned. The story is loaded up with eccentric characters, dreamlike scenes, and unforeseen changes, welcoming perusers to think about the idea of the real world and personality.

Equal universes in writing frequently act for of getting away the commonplace and encountering the unprecedented. In J.R.R. Tolkien's "The Master of the Rings," perusers are moved to Center earth, a luxuriously nitty gritty world loaded up with legendary animals, incredible clashes, and a perplexing history. Tolkien's making of an equal world isn't only a work of fiction however a completely acknowledged optional world with its own dialects, societies, and chronicles. Through this optional world, perusers can investigate subjects of chivalry, companionship, and the fight among great and insidiousness.

The idea of equal universes in writing isn't bound to the dream type. In sci-fi, creators like Philip K. Dick have investigated the possibility of various real factors and substitute aspects. Dick's book "The Man in the High Palace" presents an other history where the Hub powers won The Second Great War. The original brings up issues about the idea of truth, insight, and the outcomes of various decisions. Dick's work difficulties the customary limits of the real world and welcomes perusers to consider the "consider the possibility that" situations that equal universes offer.

Equal universes in writing are not restricted to works of fiction. Jorge Luis Borges, an expert of the brief tale, has frequently dove into the idea of equal universes. In "The Nursery of Forking Ways," Borges presents a complex story that investigates the possibility of numerous real factors and the limitless fanning of decisions. Borges' work difficulties how we might interpret time and the interconnectedness of occasions, welcoming perusers to ponder the idea of through and through freedom and fate.

Visual Craftsmanship: Mirrors and Reflections

Visual craftsmanship has likewise been a strong vehicle for the investigation of equal universes. Specialists have utilized different strategies and themes to convey substitute aspects and the transaction among the real world and deception. Perhaps of the most famous theme in craftsmanship that addresses the idea of equal universes is the mirror.

The utilization of mirrors in craftsmanship is exemplified in crafted by Dutch craftsman M.C. Escher. His popular lithograph "Relativity" portrays an existence where gravity appears to act every which way, making a maze of flights of stairs that oppose the laws of physical science. The picture difficulties how we might interpret space and viewpoint, welcoming watchers to ponder the limitless conceivable outcomes of equal universes. Escher's work frequently obscures the line between the genuine and the envisioned, provoking us to scrutinize the limits of the real world.

Surrealist specialists, including Salvador Dali and Rene Magritte, have likewise involved the mirror as an image of the psyche and the strange domains of the brain. Dali's painting "The Industriousness of Memory" highlights liquefying clocks and a desolate scene, bringing out a feeling of immortality and mutilation of the real world. Magritte's "The Foul play of Pictures" gives a line the inscription, "Ceci n'est pas une pipe" (This isn't a line), featuring the uniqueness between an item and its portrayal. These show-stoppers welcome watchers to scrutinize the idea of the real world and portrayal.

The idea of equal universes in visual craftsmanship isn't restricted to the utilization of mirrors. Craftsmen like Yayoi Kusama have made vivid establishments that transport watchers to substitute aspects. Kusama's reflected rooms and limitlessness nets offer a feeling of endless space, obscuring the limits among self and environmental elements. These establishments challenge our insights and welcome us to ponder the idea of vast conceivable outcomes.

The utilization of mirrors and appearance in craftsmanship significantly affects how we see reality. It prompts us to scrutinize the limits between the cognizant and the inner mind, the genuine and the envisioned. It urges us to investigate the transaction between oneself and the outside world. By involving mirrors as an image of equal universes, specialists make a visual exchange that connects with watchers in a consideration of the endless.

Film: Investigating the Limits of The real world

Film has likewise been a strong vehicle for the investigation of equal universes. Movie producers utilize visual and story procedures to ship crowds to substitute aspects, offering a visual and close to home experience that challenges how we might interpret reality. In film, the idea of equal universes frequently fills in for the purpose of idealism, permitting watchers to drench themselves in fantastical domains.

One of the most notable instances of equal universes in film is "The Wizard of Oz." The 1939 exemplary takes watchers on an excursion to the otherworldly place that is known for Oz, where Dorothy experiences a different cast of characters and encounters a world loaded up with dynamic tones and creative animals. The change from the sepia-conditioned Kansas to the Technicolor wonderland of Oz addresses a shift from the common to the uncommon. "The Wizard of Oz" welcomes watchers to consider the possibility that there might be equal universes ready to be found.

Equal universes in film frequently act as a representation for individual change and self-revelation. In Guillermo del Toro's "Dish's Maze," the youthful hero, Ofelia, gets away from the unforgiving real factors of post-Nationwide conflict Spain by entering a fantastical maze. Inside this equal world, she experiences legendary animals and countenances moral and moral difficulties. The film obscures the limits among the real world and dream, inciting watchers to scrutinize the idea of boldness and the groundbreaking force of creative mind.

Sci-fi films have embraced the idea of equal universes by investigating substitute aspects and different courses of events. Christopher Nolan's "Commencement" provokes the crowd to explore various layers of dreams inside dreams, each addressing an alternate reality. The film obscures the limits among dream and reality and welcomes watchers to think about the delicacy of insight.

The idea of equal universes in film has additionally led to the subgenre of the "substitute history." In films like "The Man in the High Palace" (in view of Philip K. Dick's novel) and "The Mother country," substitute history stories envision a reality where critical verifiable occasions had various results. These movies challenge how we might interpret reality by introducing situations that are both recognizable and significantly changed, provoking watchers to consider the outcomes of decisions and activities.

Movie producers have likewise utilized activity to make equal universes that challenge the imperatives of the real world. Hayao Miyazaki's "Lively Away" presents an equal reality where spirits and divine beings exist close by the human world. The film offers a luxuriously point by point and vivid experience that challenges how we might interpret the extraordinary and the interconnectedness of various domains.

Music: The Sonic Investigation of Equal Real factors

Music has the ability to ship audience members to resemble universes through the emotive and account characteristics of sound. Writers and performers frequently use music to make sonic scenes that bring out various aspects and real factors. One of the most remarkable instances of this in old style music is Gustav Holst's "The Planets," a set-up of symphonic pieces that address the visionary characteristics of the planets. Every development fills in as a melodic representation of an alternate heavenly body, offering audience members a sonic excursion through the universe. Holst's organization welcomes audience members to consider the immeasurability of the universe and the chance of powerful domains.

Electronic and exploratory music classifications have likewise embraced the idea of equal universes. Craftsmen like Brian Eno have made encompassing and generative music that drenches audience members in sonic conditions that challenge ordinary melodic designs. Eno's "Music for Air terminals" and "Music for Movies" make aural scenes that summon a feeling of powerful nature, obscuring the limits among sound and quietness.

In famous music, the idea of equal universes frequently fills in as a story gadget in idea collections and rock shows. Pink Floyd's "The Wall" is a stone drama that recounts the narrative of a hero's plummet into frenzy. The collection makes a sonic excursion through the hero's brain, offering audience members a brief look into the equal truth of his mental battles. The idea of equal universes in "The Wall" is an illustration for the hero's distance and detachment from the real world.

Chapter 9

Contemplating the Boundless Possibilities

In a world set apart by consistent change and unrelenting advancement, the human limit with regards to thought and creative mind stays a significant power forming the course of history. It is the capacity to look past the prompt skyline, to ponder the present, and to imagine the future that recognizes our species. We stand at the edge of unlimited conceivable outcomes, a domain of likely that traverses across different spaces of presence. From science and innovation to craftsmanship and reasoning, from legislative issues and society to self-awareness and self-revelation, the material of potential outcomes is immense and consistently growing.

Logical Advancement and Innovative Headways

In the domain of science and innovation, the walk of progress has been tireless. As we look forward to the year 2100, we can guess that logical disclosures and innovative progressions will keep on rethinking how we might interpret the universe and change the manner in which we live. The steady quest for information has prompted forward leaps that were once remembered to be the stuff of sci-fi.

One can consider what's on the horizon for fields like man-made consciousness (computer based intelligence) and quantum registering. The capability of artificial intelligence to alter enterprises, computerize undertakings, and even reenact human insight is striking. Quantum registering, with its capacity to handle tremendous measures of information at exceptional paces, vows to open new outskirts in tackling complex issues, from environment displaying to tranquilize disclosure.

The combination of biotechnology and nanotechnology is likewise an intriguing possibility. These fields hold the way to extraordinary progressions in medication and materials science. In 2100, we might can design tissues and organs, giving answers for organ deficiencies and upgrading human life span. Nanotechnology could empower the improvement of super light, areas of strength for super with applications in aviation, development, and endless different enterprises.

Energy is one more area with limitless potential outcomes. The change to feasible energy sources has been a main impetus in the 21st 100 years, and by 2100, environmentally friendly power advancements might have arrived at phenomenal degrees of proficiency and openness. The saddling of combination energy, a well established objective of logical examination, could give a basically boundless and clean energy source, upsetting worldwide energy creation.

Space investigation, as well, remains near the very edge of uncommon headways. In the 22nd 100 years, we might observer people laying out a long-lasting presence on Mars and wandering further into our nearby planet group. The colonization of other divine bodies could open up new roads for asset investigation and extend the limits of human progress.

Craftsmanship and Innovativeness

The universe of craftsmanship and innovativeness is similarly ready for change. As innovation keeps on advancing, it gives craftsmen new apparatuses for articulation and development. Computer generated reality and increased the truth are now modifying the manner in which we experience workmanship, considering vivid, intelligent presentations and exhibitions that rise above the limits of actual space.

Simulated intelligence produced craftsmanship has gotten forward momentum lately, bringing up issues about the idea of inventiveness and the job of the craftsman. In 2100, computer based intelligence might turn into a teammate for specialists, aiding the age of clever thoughts, plans, and sytheses. The combination of human and machine imagination could prompt a renaissance in artistic expression, pushing the limits of what is conceivable with regards to visual and hear-able articulation.

Writing and narrating may likewise go through huge changes. With progresses in simulated intelligence driven account age, we might see the rise of customized, intelligent stories that adjust to the peruser's decisions and feelings. The idea of a fixed, straight story could give way to a more liquid and dynamic narrating experience.

Philosophical Reflection

As we examine the vast potential outcomes representing things to come, reasoning will keep on assuming a urgent part in forming how we might interpret the world and our place in it. The inquiries that have enamored rationalists for quite a long time - inquiries concerning the idea of the real world, cognizance, and ethical quality - will continue, however they will be reevaluated and rethought with regards to new information and innovation.

Moral contemplations in simulated intelligence, for instance, will be of central significance. As man-made intelligence frameworks become progressively independent and equipped for pursuing moral choices, we will wrestle with inquiries concerning liability, responsibility, and the ethical ramifications of our manifestations. The advancement of man-made intelligence that can encounter abstract awareness might bring up significant issues about the idea of personhood and the moral treatment of such substances.

The combination of human and machine, whether through brain interfaces or robotic upgrades, will challenge how we might interpret human character. What's the significance here to be human in this present reality where people can alter their mental and actual capacities? Scholars will investigate the ramifications of these progressions for ideas of self, organization, and validness.

Legislative issues and Society

The social and political scene of 2100 will be molded by the interchange of worldwide difficulties and arising open doors. The continuous course of globalization, driven by propels in correspondence and transportation, will keep on obscuring the limits among countries and societies. It is inside this setting that we should consider the endless opportunities for administration, collaboration, and cultural change.

Quite possibly of the most major problem in the 21st century has been environmental change, and its belongings will keep on resonating into the 22nd 100 years. Be that as it may, the unfathomable potential outcomes of innovation offer expect alleviating the effects of environmental change. High level environmentally friendly power arrangements, carbon catch innovations, and geoengineering may hold the keys to a supportable future.

The idea of a worldwide government or worldwide administration designs might get some decent momentum as countries face progressively related difficulties. Worldwide establishments and arrangements could advance to resolve issues like environmental change, pandemics, and asset the executives. The chance of worldwide citizenship and a more comprehensive world request is a tempting possibility, however it accompanies its own arrangement of difficulties and intricacies.

A majority rules system and administration might go through critical changes. Propels in data innovation, blockchain, and secure democratic frameworks might prompt more straightforward and participatory types of direction, possibly diminishing the impact of middle people and improving straightforwardness. The harmony between individual opportunities and aggregate prosperity will keep on being a focal topic in political talk.

Cultural changes will likewise be driven by shifts in socioeconomics, with maturing populaces and changing family structures reshaping the social texture. The job of work and work might be reclassified as robotization and artificial intelligence take on additional errands, prompting conversations about all inclusive essential pay, recreation, and the quest for significant exercises.

Self-awareness and Self-Disclosure

In the midst of the immense range of outer conceivable outcomes, the excursion of self-disclosure and self-improvement stays a getting through human mission. In the year 2100, people might approach a phenomenal cluster of apparatuses and assets for grasping themselves and understanding their true capacity.

Headways in neuroscience and brain science might offer new bits of knowledge into the idea of cognizance and the human psyche. Strategies for mental upgrade and mental prosperity could become typical, prompting more satisfied and self-completed people. The investigation of adjusted conditions of cognizance, whether through contemplation, computer generated reality, or neurotechnology, may open up new components of human experience.

The convergence of innovation and self-awareness is now clear in the ascent of computerized self improvement applications, wearable gadgets that track wellbeing and health, and the prospering field of life training controlled by computer based intelligence. In 2100, these apparatuses may turn out to be significantly more modern, giving fitted direction and backing to people endeavoring to accomplish their objectives and upgrade their general prosperity.

The subject of leading a significant and satisfying life will keep on being a subject of thought. As the limits of customary normal practices and profession ways obscure, people might have the opportunity to characterize their own ways and purposes. Methods of reasoning of bliss and prosperity might develop, underscoring the significance of connections, local area, and self-awareness.

8.1 Reflection on the journey of exploration

The human soul is an inquisitive and bold one, continuously longing to push the limits of information, to investigate the obscure, and to look for figuring out despite the huge secrets that encompass us. From the earliest days of our reality, people have been driven by a steady craving to investigate the world, both on The planet and then some. As we ponder the excursion of investigation, it becomes obvious that it has been a characterizing element of our species, molding how we might interpret the universe and our place inside it.

Investigation on The planet

The excursion of investigation started on our own planet, as early people branched out of their familial countries to find new regions and assets. It was a basic journey for endurance, driven by the need to track down food and haven. Over the long haul, this sense for investigation developed into a social and scholarly undertaking, prompting the revelation of different scenes, societies, and environments.

The investigations of old human advancements, like the Phoenicians, Greeks, and Polynesians, were instrumental in extending our insight into the World's geology. These early sailors diagrammed obscure waters, associated far off lands, and exchanged products, accordingly establishing the groundworks for the improvement of human civilizations. Their processes were portrayed by mental fortitude, interest, and a longing to interface with others.

The Time of Revelation, spreading over the fifteenth to the seventeenth hundreds of years, denoted an extraordinary period in mankind's set of experiences. European wayfarers, driven by a hunger for riches, information, and the spread of their realms, set forth on trying journeys that would redirect history. Christopher Columbus, Vasco da Gama, and Ferdinand Magellan are among the renowned voyagers of this time, who extended the well explored parts of the planet through their oceanic undertakings. These wayfarers not just found new terrains, like the Americas, yet additionally settled shipping lanes that worked with social trades among East and West.

The longing to investigate was not restricted to the oceans. Land-based investigations likewise assumed an imperative part in growing comprehension we might interpret the world. The Silk Street, an old organization of shipping lanes that associated East and West, took into consideration the trading of products, thoughts, and societies. It worked with the progression of information and innovations, changing social orders and cultivating a feeling of worldwide interconnectedness.

Investigation in the cutting edge time stretched out past topography. Logical investigation turned into a focal undertaking, driven by a craving to figure out the regular world. The journeys of Charles Darwin on the HMS Beagle and the examination of naturalists like Alexander von Humboldt prompted earth shattering revelations in the areas of science and environment. These pilgrims exposed the unimaginable variety of life on The planet and the interconnectedness of environments.

The twentieth century denoted another section in investigation with the victory of the skies. The Wright siblings' originally controlled trip in 1903 made the way for another domain of disclosure. Flying trailblazers like Amelia Earhart and Charles Lindbergh pushed the limits of what was conceivable in the air. Their accomplishments caught the creative mind of individuals overall and denoted the beginning of the advanced period of aeronautics.

Space Investigation

While earthbound investigation had been a focal concentration for centuries, the twentieth century saw the beginning of another outskirts - space investigation. The investigation of room addresses one of the most amazing and daring excursions in mankind's set of experiences. It represents our natural interest and our tenacious journey to appreciate the universe.

The send off of Sputnik 1 by the Soviet Association in 1957 denoted the start of the space age. It was a groundbreaking second, as humankind wandered past the bounds of Earth's air and into the immense span of room. This spearheading accomplishment was trailed by the memorable Apollo 11 mission in 1969 when people previously set foot on the moon. Space explorers Neil Armstrong and Buzz Aldrin's lunar landing was a groundbreaking occasion that caught the world's consideration, exhibiting mankind's ability to achieve the apparently inconceivable.

The investigation of room has prompted significant logical disclosures and progressions. Telescopes, similar to the Hubble Space Telescope, have given extraordinary experiences into the far off ranges of the universe, uncovering cosmic systems, nebulae, and heavenly peculiarities that were already inconceivable. Space missions to far off planets and moons, like the Explorer missions and the Mars wanderers, have extended how we might interpret the planetary group and the potential for life past Earth.

The Worldwide Space Station (ISS), a cooperative task including numerous countries, has given a stage to logical examination in microgravity, offering bits of knowledge into the impacts of long-length spaceflight on the human body and cultivating global collaboration in the investigation of room. The ISS has likewise filled in as a venturing stone for future missions to the Moon, Mars, and then some.

Mars has turned into a point of convergence of interest lately. Different missions have been sent off to investigate the Red Planet, looking for proof of past or present life and getting ready for likely human colonization. The fantasy of people going to Mars, similar as they did on the moon, addresses a tempting possibility for the fate of room investigation.

The quest for exoplanets, planets situated external our planetary group, has likewise picked up speed. With the revelation of thousands of exoplanets, researchers are reducing the opportunities for tracking down other tenable universes and possibly indications of extraterrestrial life. The James Webb Space Telescope, scheduled for send off, vows to reform how we might interpret the universe by concentrating on the airs and creations of exoplanets.

While space investigation has progressed our logical information, it has additionally caught the human creative mind. Venturing out to far off stars, investigating the universe, and experiencing insightful extraterrestrial life has been a wellspring of motivation for sci-fi, writing, and mainstream society. The opportunities for interstellar travel and correspondence with different civilizations, while presently the stuff of fiction, stay a wellspring of thought and marvel.

Challenges and Moral Contemplations

The excursion of investigation, whether on The planet or in space, has not been without its difficulties and moral contemplations. As people wandered into new regions, they experienced native populaces, frequently bringing about social conflicts, clashes, and the abuse of native people groups. The historical backdrop of investigation is damaged by imperialism and the abuse of assets, which had enduring and frequently decimating ramifications for native networks.

In space investigation, inquiries of moral obligation emerge also. The potential for defiling other divine bodies with Earth's microorganisms, as well as the chance of finding extraterrestrial life, raises significant moral issues. How might we deal with these revelations, and what obligations do we need to safeguard the uprightness of different biological systems, whether on The planet or in space?

Natural worries are likewise a pivotal part of investigation. The natural effect of human exercises, like space trash and contamination, can possibly influence both our planet and the divine bodies we visit. Mindful investigation requests that we consider the drawn out results of our activities and do whatever it takes to limit our effect on the conditions we experience.

Notwithstanding moral contemplations, the monetary expenses of investigation are a critical test. Space missions, specifically, can be restrictively costly, and state run administrations and space offices should adjust the longing for investigation with the need to designate assets for other basic necessities, like medical care, schooling, and social administrations. The contribution of privately owned businesses in space investigation has opened additional opportunities for funding and development, however it likewise raises worries about business intrigues overshadowing the benefit of all.

The excursion of investigation isn't without chances, by the same token. Space investigation, specifically, conveys inborn risks, from the dangers of send off and reemergence to the perils of profound space. The deficiency of space travelers and shuttle is an unmistakable indication of the mental fortitude and penance expected to push the limits of our insight.

The Eventual fate of Investigation

As we think about the fate of investigation, it is clear that the excursion is nowhere near finished. The human soul of interest and revelation keeps on driving us to new skylines and conceivable outcomes. The following century holds incredible commitment for investigation, with a mix of innovative headways and a developing consciousness of the significance of mindful investigation.

Earth-bound investigation will keep on growing comprehension we might interpret our planet's biological systems, biodiversity, and environment. The investigation of remote ocean environments, unknown rainforests, and far off mountain reaches will divulge new species and biological connections, prompting bits of knowledge that can illuminate preservation endeavors and economical turn of events. The utilization of robots, independent vehicles, and high level planning advances will upgrade our capacity to investigate and concentrate on Earth's most remote and difficult to reach locales.

Space investigation, as well, will encounter noteworthy turns of events. The vision of people going to Mars and laying out a maintainable presence on the moon is a tempting possibility that might turn into a reality in the next few decades. Progresses in impetus innovation, life emotionally supportive networks, and reasonable natural surroundings will be crucial for make these desires a reality. Global collaboration will be pivotal in pooling assets and ability to accomplish these aggressive objectives.

8.2 The interconnectedness of events and choices

The embroidery of life is woven from a huge number of occasions, decisions, and conditions that shape the course of our singular processes and the aggregate way of humankind. Each second in our lives is impacted by a perplexing snare of interconnected factors, both interior and outside. Our decisions and the situation that develop are inseparably connected, making a dynamic and steadily developing scene. As we dig into the significant complexities of this interconnectedness, we can acquire a more profound comprehension of how our activities echo through reality, influencing ourselves as well as our general surroundings.

Individual Decisions and Outcomes

At the core of the interconnectedness of occasions and decisions lies the person. Every individual is a nexus of choices, contemplations, and activities that straightforwardly affect their life and the existences of people around them. Our own decisions, both huge and little, put into high gear a chain of occasions that can have expansive results.

Consider the choice to seek after a specific vocation way. This decision might prompt a progression of occasions, including instructive pursuits, open positions, and expert connections. Over the long run, it can shape not exclusively one's very own prosperity yet in addition their commitment to the economy and society. A choice to turn into a specialist, for instance, can bring about a profession of recuperating and saving lives, at last influencing the wellbeing and prosperity of endless people.

Similarly, individual decisions can impact the climate. Choices about way of life, utilization, and transportation have an immediate bearing on fossil fuel byproducts and environmental change. Every decision to lessen, reuse, or reuse adds to the supportability of the planet. Alternately, decisions that focus on comfort and inefficiency can fuel ecological difficulties.

The interconnectedness of occasions and decisions is apparent in the domain of individual connections too. A choice to keep up with or cut off a kinship can set off a chain of occasions that resonates through the existences of the two people and their more extensive groups of friends. The expanding influence of these decisions is felt sincerely as well as in the texture of our social associations.

The idea of "the butterfly impact" outlines the significant interconnectedness of individual decisions and occasions. This representation, frequently connected with turmoil hypothesis, places that the fold of a butterfly's wings in a single region of the planet can get under way a succession of occasions that prompts a typhoon in one more region of the planet. While the similarity might be to some degree exaggerated, it highlights that apparently immaterial activities can have broad results.

Verifiable Occasions and Cultural Decisions

Zooming out from the singular level, we observe that the interconnectedness of occasions and decisions is similarly pertinent with regards to history and society. The aggregate selections of social orders, legislatures, and organizations shape the direction of whole civic establishments, making a permanent imprint on the course of mankind's set of experiences.

The results of major verifiable occasions frequently depend on a grouping of decisions made by pioneers and social orders. The flare-up of The Second Great War, for instance, was the perfection of perplexing international choices, coalitions, and clashes. The results of this conflict, including the Settlement of Versailles and the redrawing of public limits, laid the preparation for The Second Great War and the ensuing rebuilding of the world request.

The decisions made by states can significantly affect the prosperity of their residents. Social strategies, financial choices, and medical services drives all impact the personal satisfaction for people inside a general public. The execution of all inclusive medical care, for example, can further develop admittance to clinical benefits, advance by and large wellbeing, and decrease monetary weights on residents.

Monetary decisions, like tax collection approaches and economic accords, can either prod monetary development or lead to monetary emergencies. The worldwide monetary emergency of 2008 was a consequence of interconnected decisions made by monetary establishments, controllers, and states. The repercussions of this emergency were felt around the world, with employment misfortunes, real estate market slumps, and financial downturns influencing a huge number of people.

Ecological decisions at the cultural level have worldwide ramifications. Choices connected with deforestation, petroleum derivative utilization, and modern contamination have added to environmental change and its related outcomes, including outrageous climate occasions, rising ocean levels, and the relocation of populaces. The decisions made by social orders to moderate or intensify ecological difficulties have an immediate bearing on the strength of the planet and people in the future.

The interconnectedness of occasions and decisions stretches out to civil rights and social equality. Verifiable developments, like the social liberties development in the US, were driven by the aggregate selections of people who tried to challenge foundational separation and disparity. The endeavors of activists, joined with lawful and authoritative changes, have changed social orders and affected the course of social advancement.

Worldwide Occasions and Global Decisions

The worldwide stage amplifies the intricacy of interconnected occasions and decisions. As countries communicate and work together on worldwide issues, the decisions can have significant ramifications for worldwide steadiness, harmony, and thriving. The world has seen the interconnectedness of occasions and decisions in regions like tact, exchange, and security.

Conciliatory decisions, especially those connected with compromise and harmony discussions, have the ability to forestall or heighten equipped struggles. The decision to take part in discretionary exchange and look for tranquil goals to questions can deflect the detestations of war. On the other hand, choices to seek after forceful military activities can prompt struggle, relocation, and human anguish.

The interconnectedness of occasions and decisions is obviously clear in global exchange. Worldwide economic accords, taxes, and monetary arrangements impact the progression of merchandise, the dependability of economies, and the jobs of laborers. Choices to take part in protectionist exchange measures, for example, can upset worldwide stock chains and trigger retaliatory activities, affecting businesses and economies across borders.

Worldwide wellbeing emergencies, for example, the Coronavirus pandemic, highlight the relationship of countries and their decisions in light of shared difficulties. The choices of states with respect to travel limitations, immunization conveyance, and medical care foundation can influence the spread of irresistible infections and the prosperity of populaces around the world.

Security decisions and unions likewise assume a basic part in the interconnectedness of occasions. Military unions, safeguard arrangements, and the utilization of power because of dangers are interconnected decisions that have an immediate bearing on worldwide security. The North Atlantic Settlement Association (NATO) and its shared guard responsibility, for instance, mirror the interconnected decisions of part countries to guarantee aggregate security.

The Unified Countries, as a gathering for worldwide participation, epitomizes the interconnectedness of occasions and decisions on a worldwide scale. Choices made inside the UN system, like goals on peacekeeping missions, philanthropic mediations, and worldwide advancement objectives, mirror the cooperative endeavors of countries to address shared difficulties and potential open doors.

Natural issues, for example, environmental change and biodiversity preservation, are quintessential instances of the interconnectedness of occasions and decisions at the worldwide level. The decisions made by countries to lessen ozone depleting substance outflows, safeguard regular environments, and advance maintainable practices straightforwardly affect the soundness of the planet and the conservation of biological systems that rise above public lines.

The Job of Innovation and Data

In the cutting edge time, innovation and data play had a vital impact in enhancing the interconnectedness of occasions and decisions. The quick trade of data through computerized stages and the web has made a worldwide interconnectedness that was beforehand inconceivable.

The ascent of virtual entertainment, specifically, has changed how data is scattered and has given people and networks a voice on the worldwide stage. The decisions to share news, conclusions, and encounters via virtual entertainment stages can prompt the fast spread of data, affecting popular assessment and forming talk on different issues.

The effect of innovation on interconnected occasions and decisions reaches out to regions like business and trade. Internet business, for example, has changed shopper conduct, empowering people to settle on decisions about items and administrations from around the world with a couple of snaps. Mechanical advancements, like computerized reasoning and mechanization, have additionally impacted the options made by organizations in regards to labor force and creation strategies.

Progressions in correspondence innovation have obscured the limits among nearby and worldwide occasions, making it workable for people to be educated about occasions happening in far off regions of the planet continuously. This instantaneousness has prompted more prominent consciousness of worldwide issues, affecting decisions connected with compassionate guide, activism, and calamity reaction.

Nonetheless, the interconnectedness worked with by innovation likewise presents difficulties, including issues of security, online protection, and the spread of disinformation. The decisions made by people, associations, and states with respect to the utilization of innovation can have suggestions for security, morals, and cultural prosperity.

8.3 The enduring quest for understanding the mysteries of the cosmos

All through the records of mankind's set of experiences, a getting through mission has driven our species to gaze toward the night sky and contemplate the secrets of the universe. From the earliest civic establishments to the current day, the human quest for information about the universe has risen above time and social limits. This tireless interest in the universe has prompted significant logical revelations, creative articulations, and philosophical examinations. An excursion keeps on forming how we might interpret the universe and our place inside it.

The Beginning of Cosmology

The narrative of mankind's journey to comprehend the universe starts with the earliest civic establishments. For centuries, the night sky filled in as a wellspring of marvel and motivation, as well as an aide for route, timekeeping, and schedule frameworks. Old societies all over the planet, from the Egyptians and Babylonians to the Maya and Chinese, created complicated cosmological models and fantasies to make sense of the developments of heavenly bodies.

One of the most notorious accomplishments of old stargazing was the development of Stonehenge, a Neolithic landmark in Britain, which filled in as a cosmic observatory and schedule. The arrangement of its stones with key divine occasions, like solstices and lunar stages, verifies the antiquated human interest with the sky.

The rise of Greek way of thinking and logical idea in the sixth century BCE denoted a huge defining moment in the journey for enormous comprehension. The Greek rationalist Anaximander proposed a cosmological model in which heavenly bodies were suspended in concentric rings, while Pythagoras and his devotees examined the numerical underpinnings of the universe.

Notwithstanding, it was crafted by rationalists like Aristotle and stargazers like Claudius Ptolemy that molded the predominant cosmological model of the old world. Ptolemy's geocentric model, as expressed in his "Almagest," held influence for quite a long time, placing that the Earth was at the focal point of the universe, with divine bodies moving in complex epicyclic circles.

The Copernican Transformation and Then some

The Copernican Unrest, lighted by the distribution of Nicolaus Copernicus' "De revolutionibus orbium coelestium" in 1543, tested the geocentric perspective on the universe. Copernicus' heliocentric model set the Sun at the focal point of the planetary group, preparing for a significant change in cosmology and our comprehension of heavenly movement.

Crafted by Johannes Kepler and his laws of planetary movement, alongside Galileo Galilei's adjustable perceptions, gave additional proof to the heliocentric model and laid out the establishment for current space science. Galileo's perceptions of the periods of Venus and the moons of Jupiter straightforwardly tested the geocentric view, and he was subsequently positioned detained at home by the Catholic Church for his sinful thoughts.

The getting through mission for understanding the universe was set apart by one more critical second with the distribution of Sir Isaac Newton's "Philosophiæ Naturalis Principia Mathematica" in 1687. Newton's laws of movement and widespread attractive energy joined heavenly and earthly material science, exhibiting the force of arithmetic in depicting the elements of the universe.

The introduction of present day cosmology was additionally cutting-edge by stargazers like Johannes Hevelius, Edmond Halley, and Charles More chaotic, who recorded the positions and developments of divine articles. The advancement of progressively strong telescopes extended humankind's perspective on the universe, disclosing the presence of nebulae, worlds, and the limitlessness of the universe.

The Exquisite Universe and the Speculations of Relativity

The twentieth century introduced another period of vast comprehension with the improvement of Albert Einstein's hypothesis of extraordinary relativity in 1905. This pivotal hypothesis tested old style thoughts of existence, uncovering the exchange between mass, energy, and the speed of light. Exceptional relativity on a very basic level changed the structure of traditional physical science and laid the preparation for Einstein's later hypothesis of general relativity.

Einstein's hypothesis of general relativity, distributed in 1915, presented the idea of spacetime arch, by which mass and energy twist the texture of the universe. The hypothesis gave a clever clarification to the power of gravity, setting that monstrous items cause spacetime to twist, making the gravitational fascination experienced by different items.

One of the most commended expectations of general relativity was the bowing of light by gravity, which was affirmed during the 1919 sun oriented obscure. The English space expert Sir Arthur Eddington drove a campaign to notice the twisting of starlight as it passed close to the Sun, approving Einstein's hypothesis and catapulting him to global acclaim.

Einstein's hypotheses of relativity likewise prompted the expectation of dark openings, areas in spacetime where the gravitational force is extreme to the point that nothing, not even light, can get away. Dark openings, albeit at first saw as numerical interests, have since turned into a focal point of astrophysical exploration, with their reality upheld by an abundance of observational proof.

The hypothesis of general relativity essentially modified how we might interpret the universe, offering another structure for figuring out the gravitational cooperations between divine bodies. It has since assumed a significant part in the investigation of the extension of the universe, the development of worlds, and the elements of grandiose designs.

Cosmological Secrets and the Huge explosion

Perhaps of the most significant inquiry in cosmology concerns the beginning of the actual universe. The journey to comprehend the grandiose starting points prompted the improvement of the Theory of how things came to be. Georges Lemaître, a Belgian cleric and physicist, proposed the hypothesis during the 1920s, recommending that the universe had an unmistakable start and had been extending from that point onward.

The idea of a growing universe was upheld by crafted by American cosmologist Edwin Hubble, who noticed the redshift of light from far off worlds. The redshift, characteristic of the movement of worlds from us, gave observational proof to the extension of the universe and loaned solid help to the Theory of prehistoric cosmic detonation.

The persevering through mission for understanding the secrets of the universe took a goliath jump forward during the twentieth 100 years with the revelation of the inestimable microwave foundation radiation.

Arno Penzias and Robert Wilson, radio space experts at Chime Labs, recognized a weak, uniform foundation radiation penetrating the universe. This disclosure gave solid proof to the Theory of how things came to be, as the grandiose microwave foundation radiation is a leftover of the universe's initial, incredibly hot state.

The Theory of how things came to be places that the universe rose up out of a peculiarity, a boundlessly thick and hot point, roughly 13.8 quite a while back. As the universe extended, it cooled, leading to the development of issue, systems, and the huge grandiose designs we notice today.